This Book Belongs to:

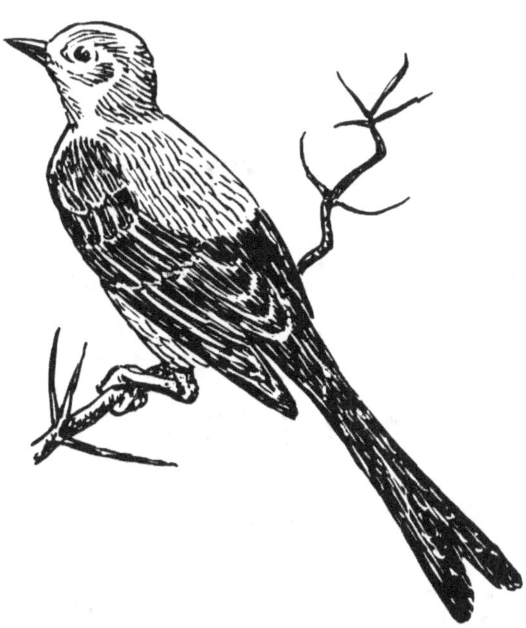

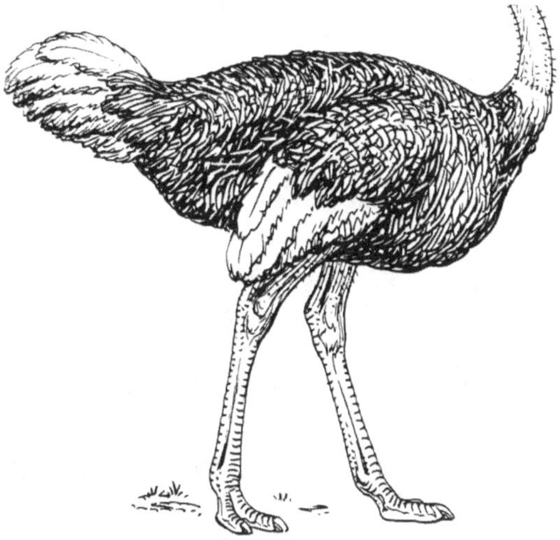

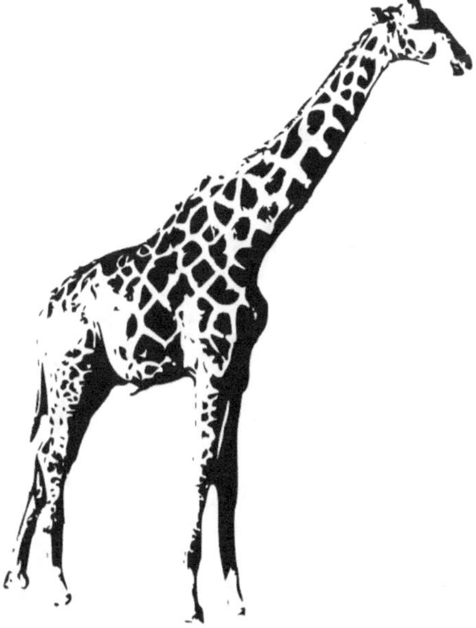

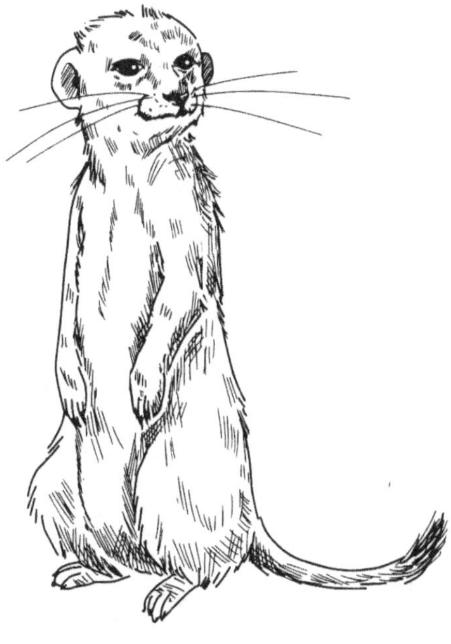

Test Color Page

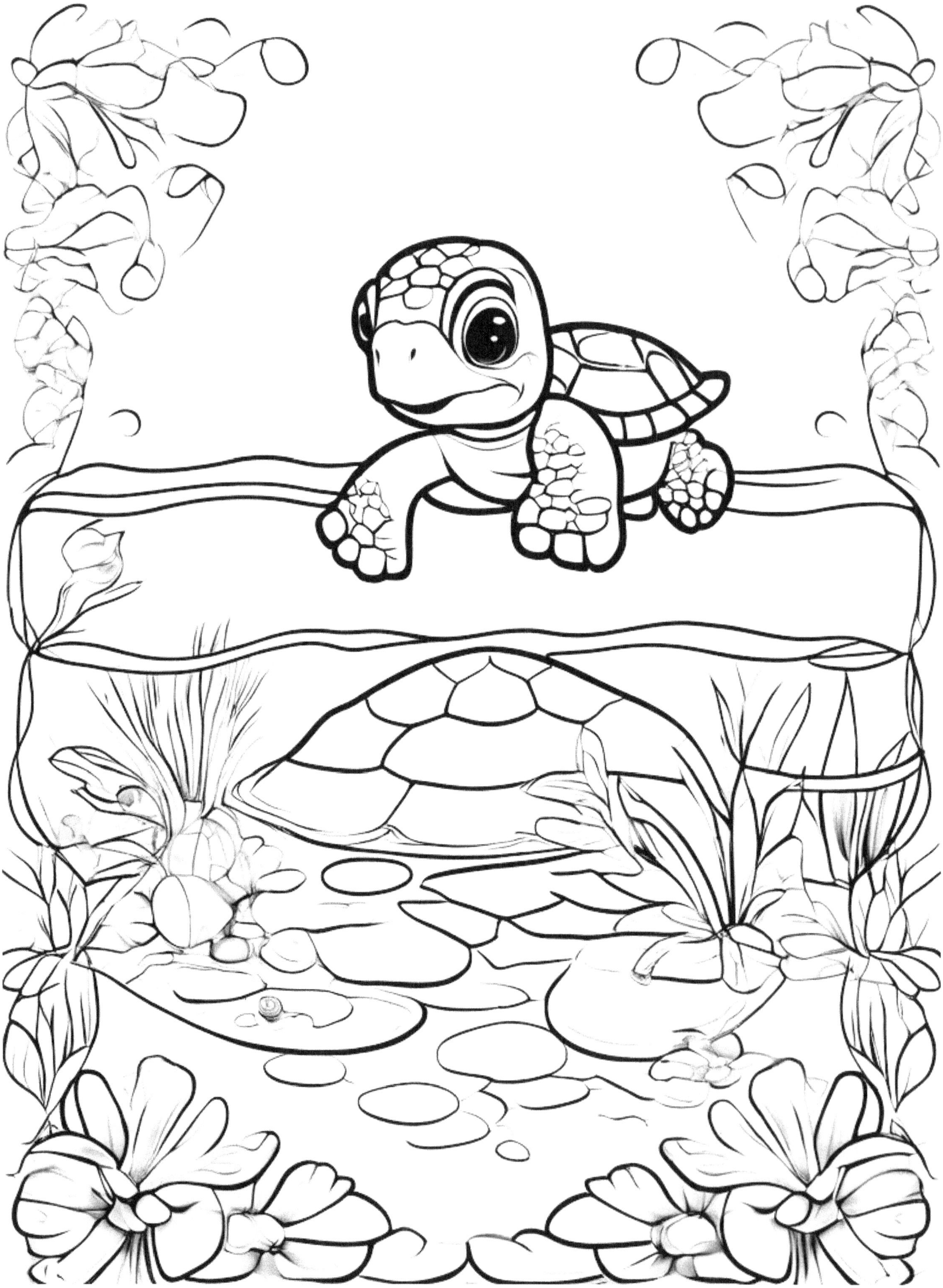

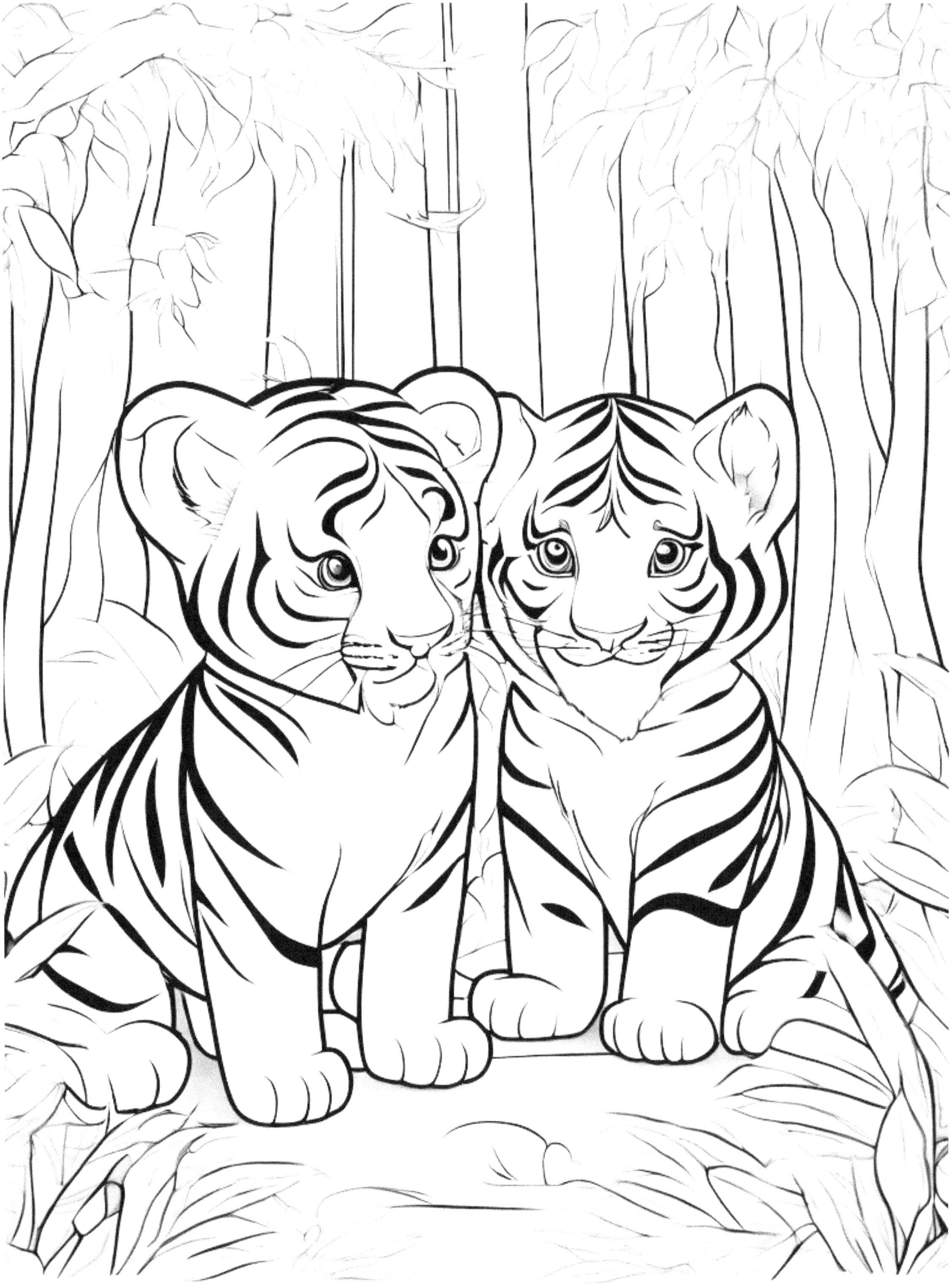

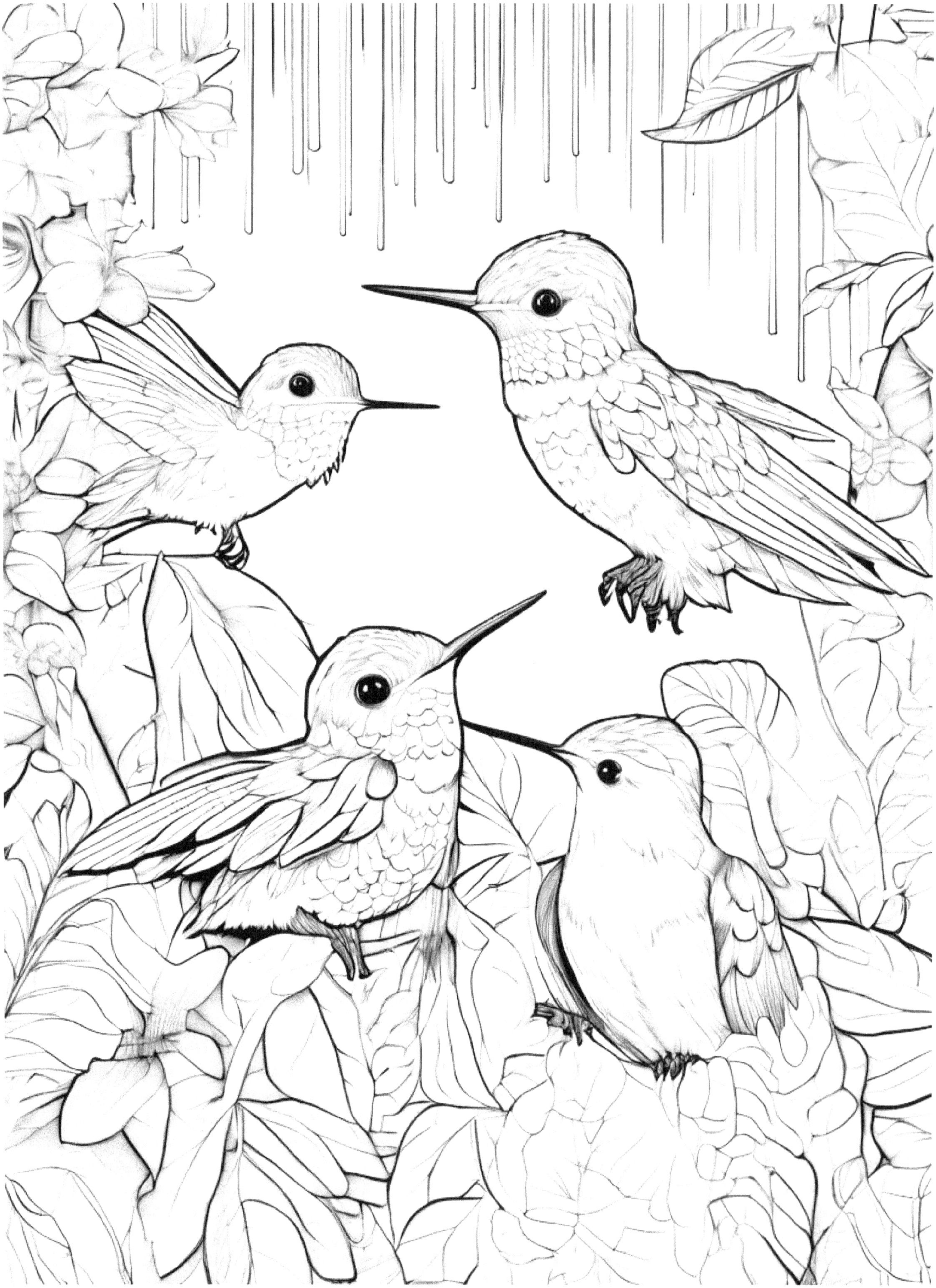

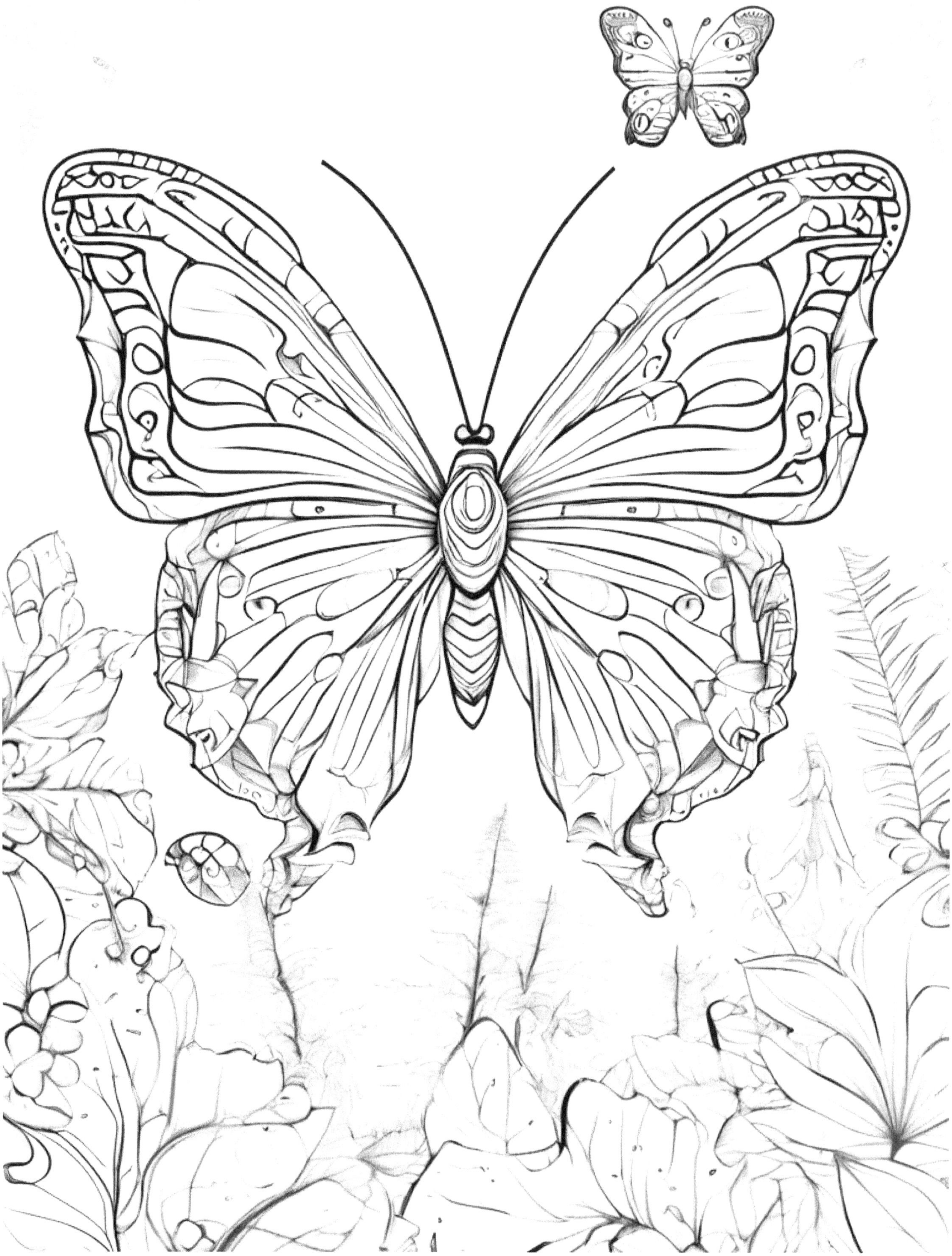

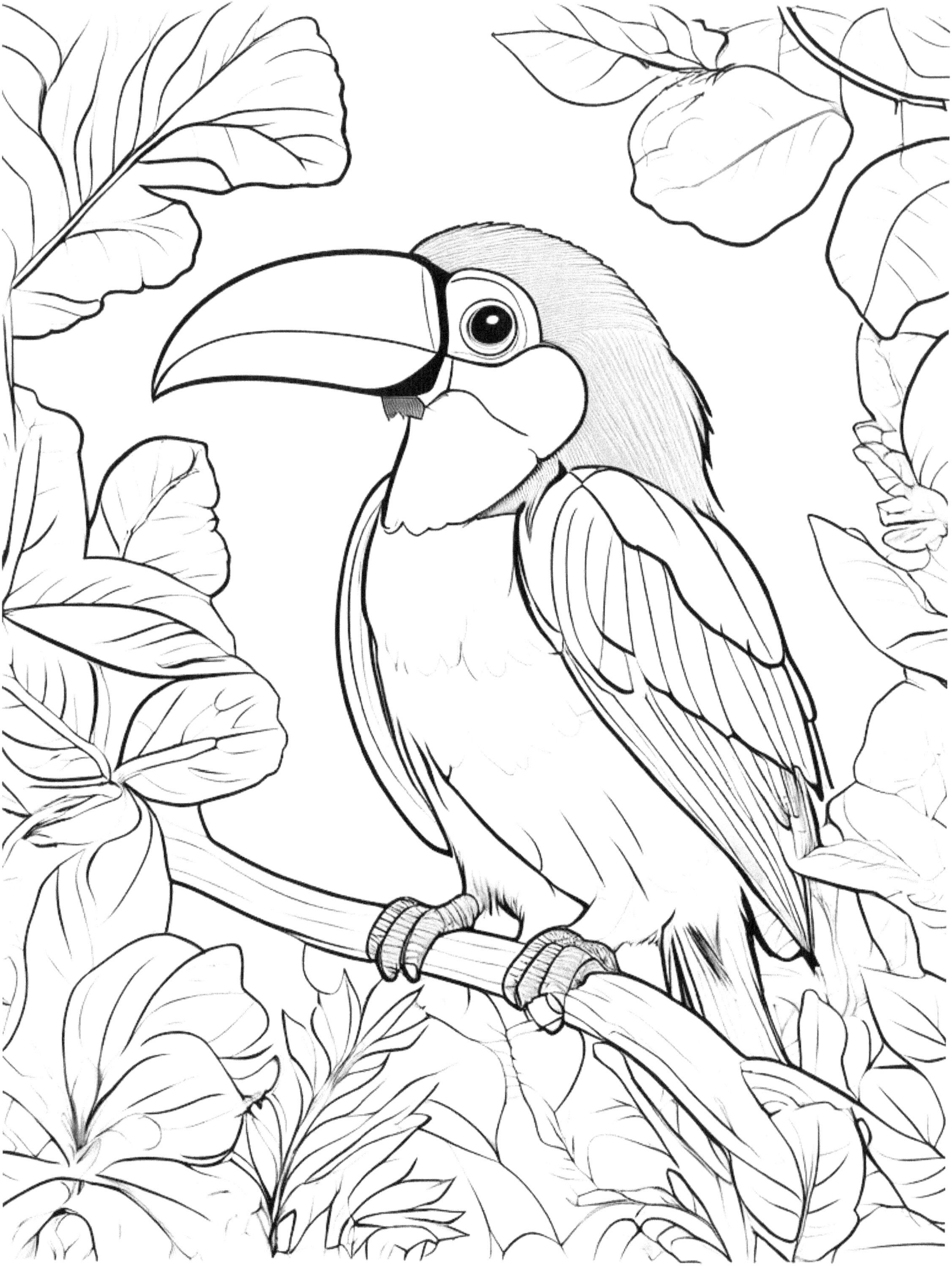

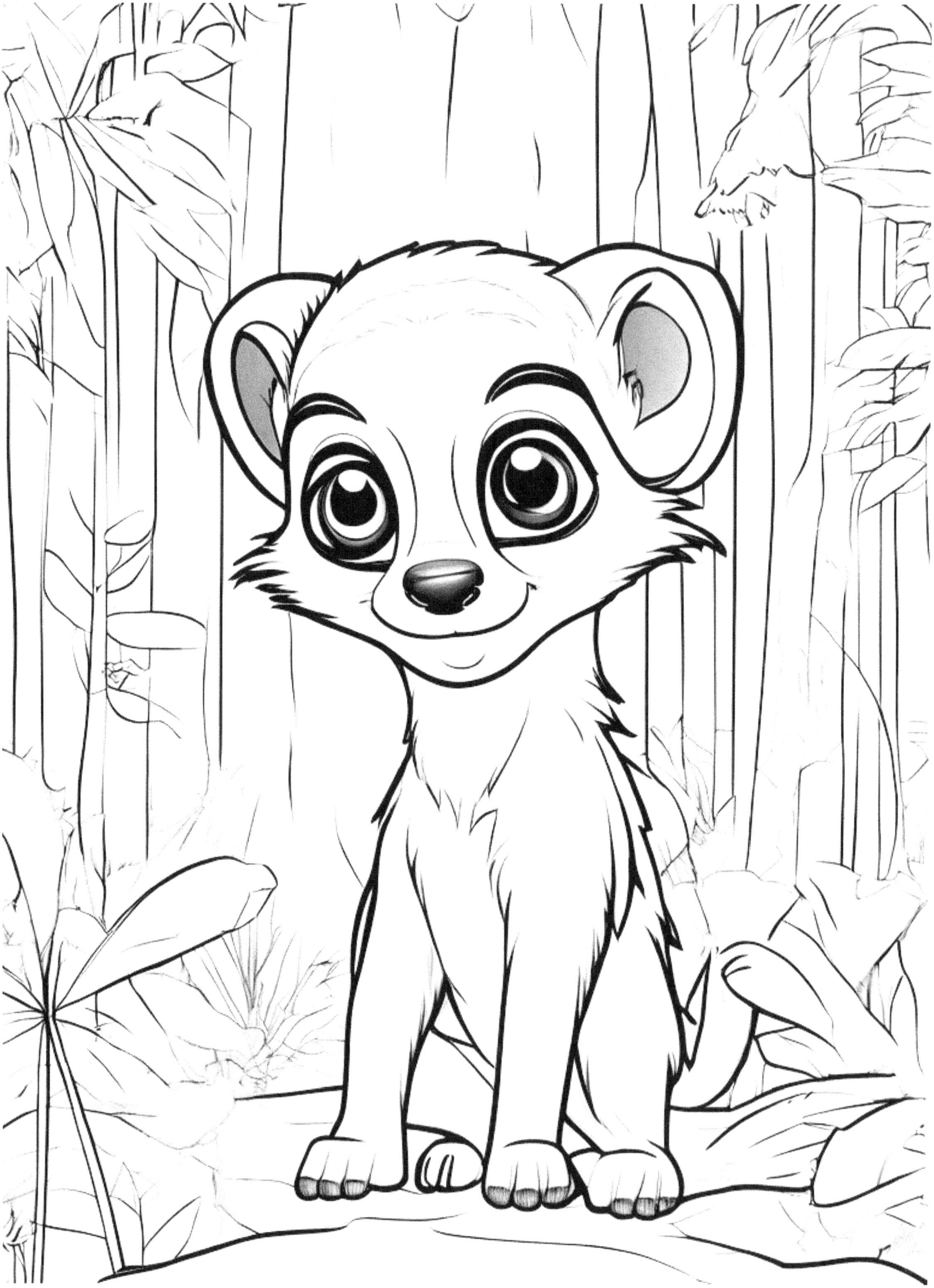

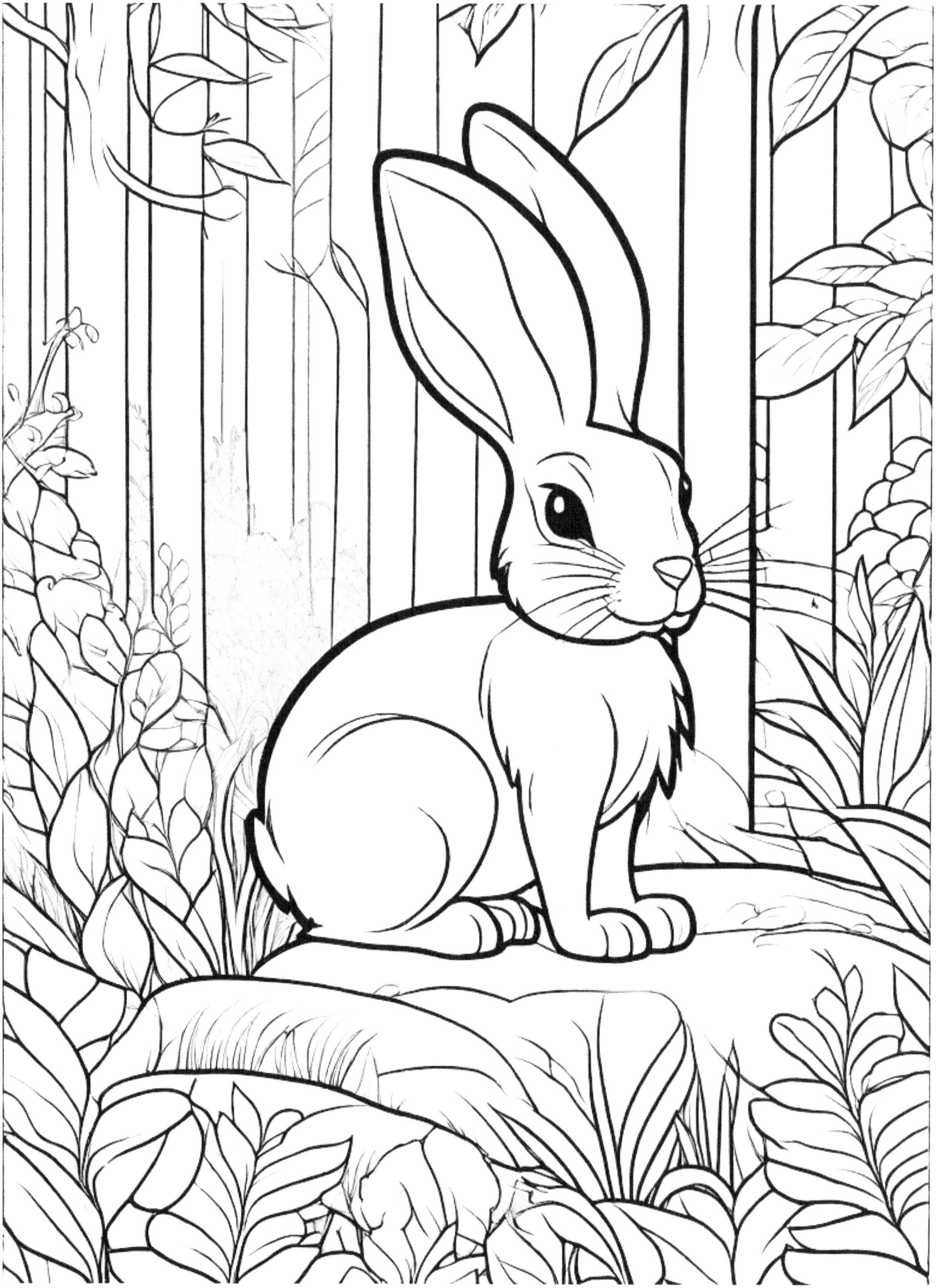

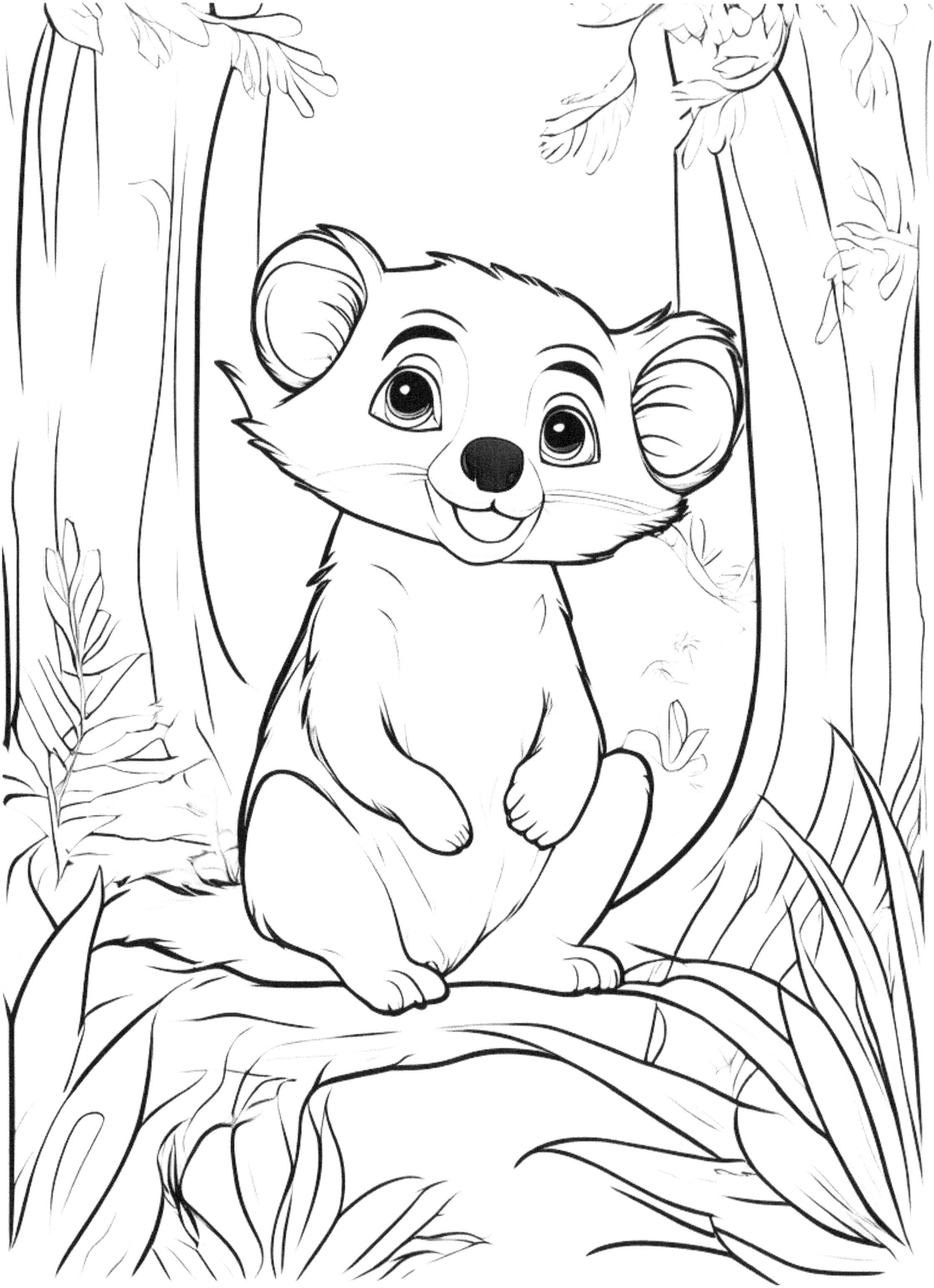

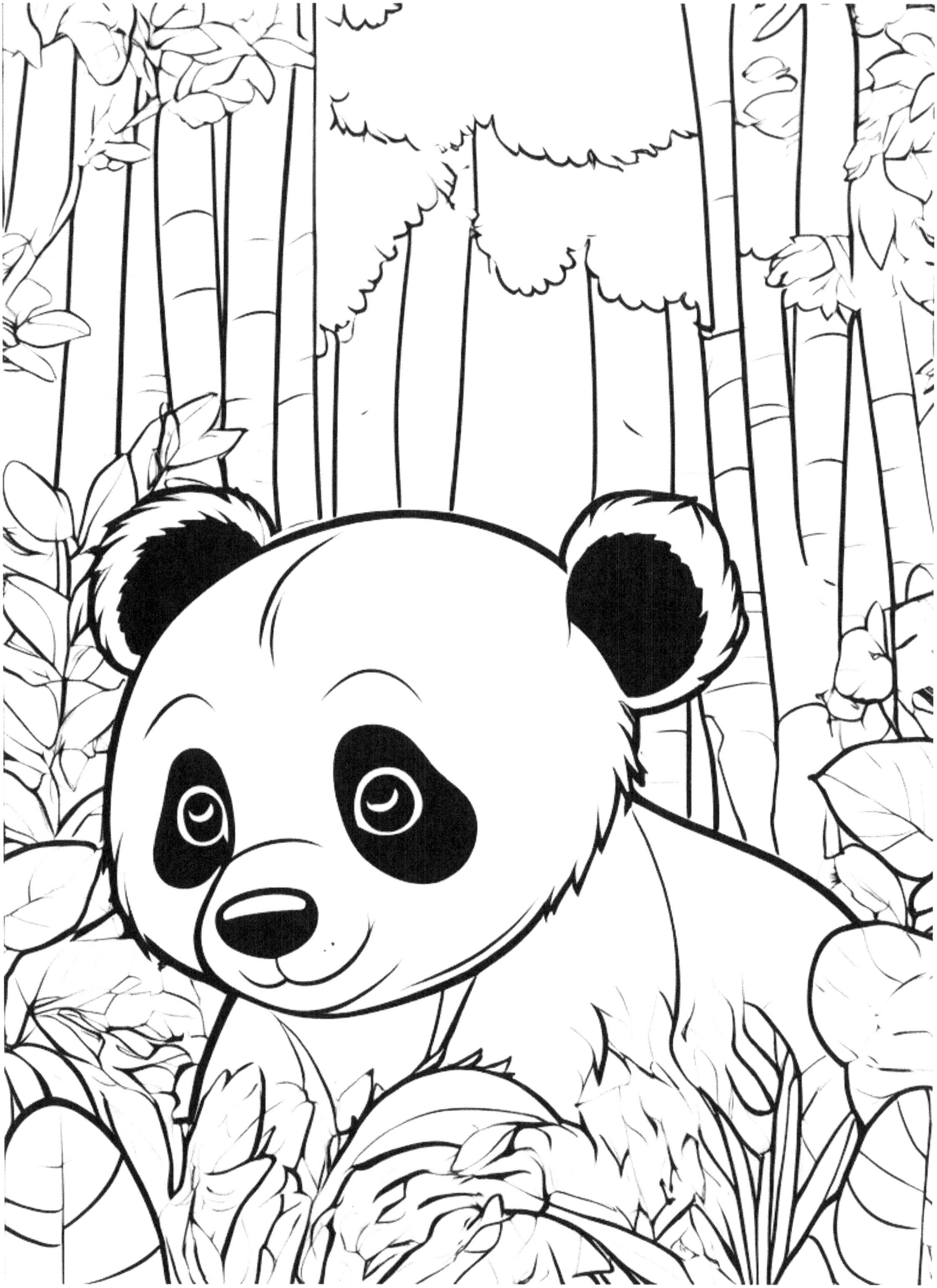

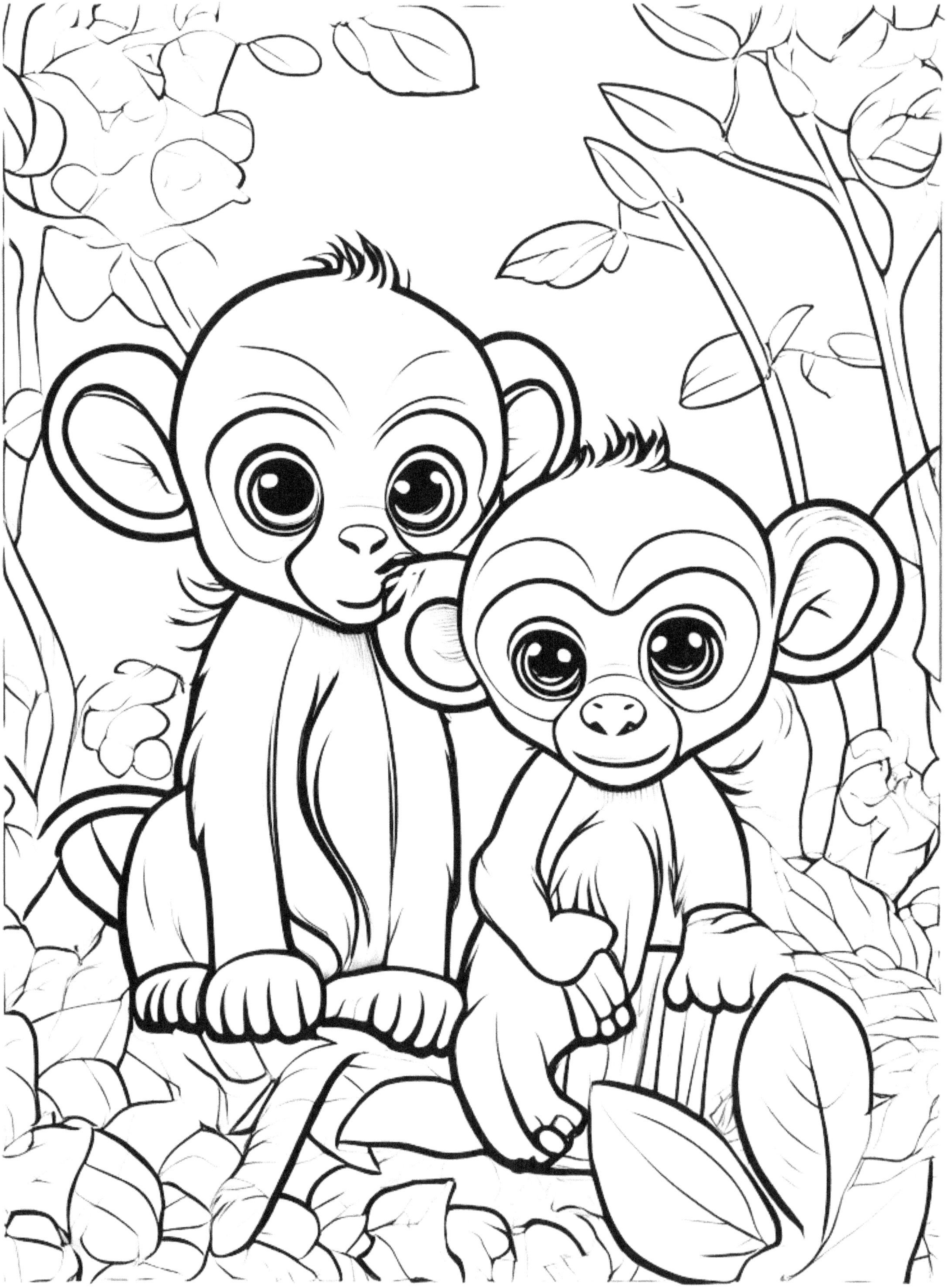

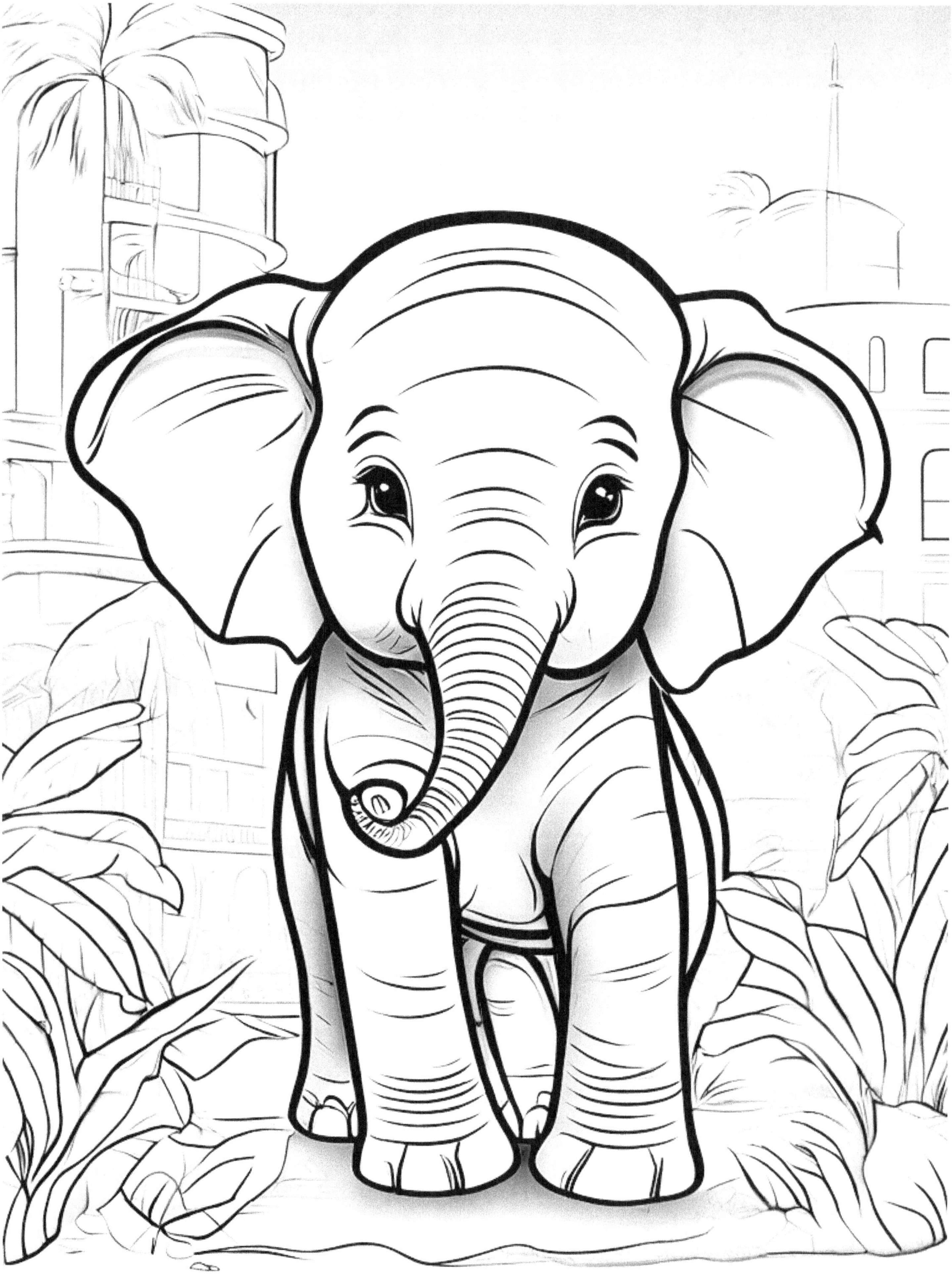

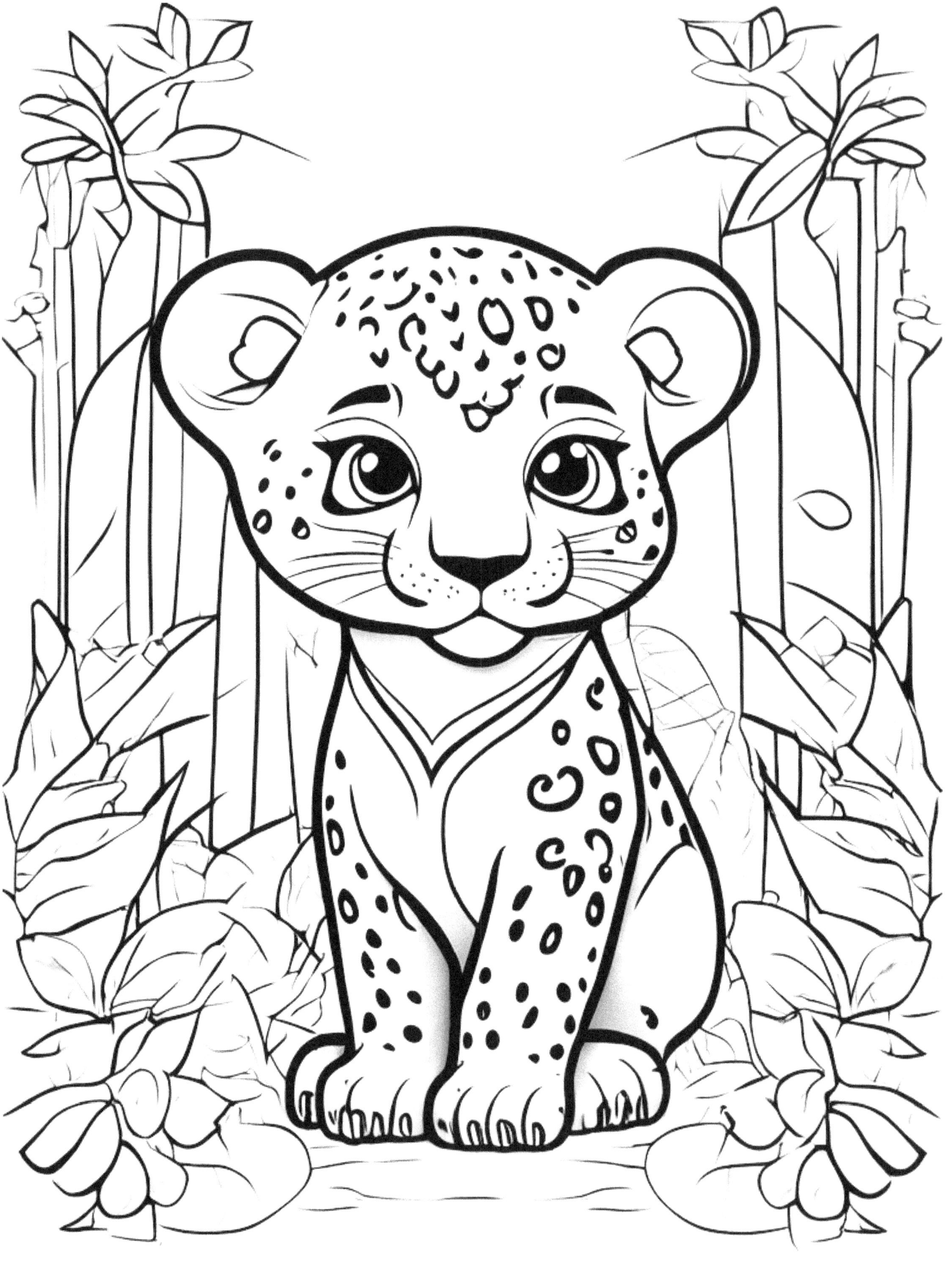

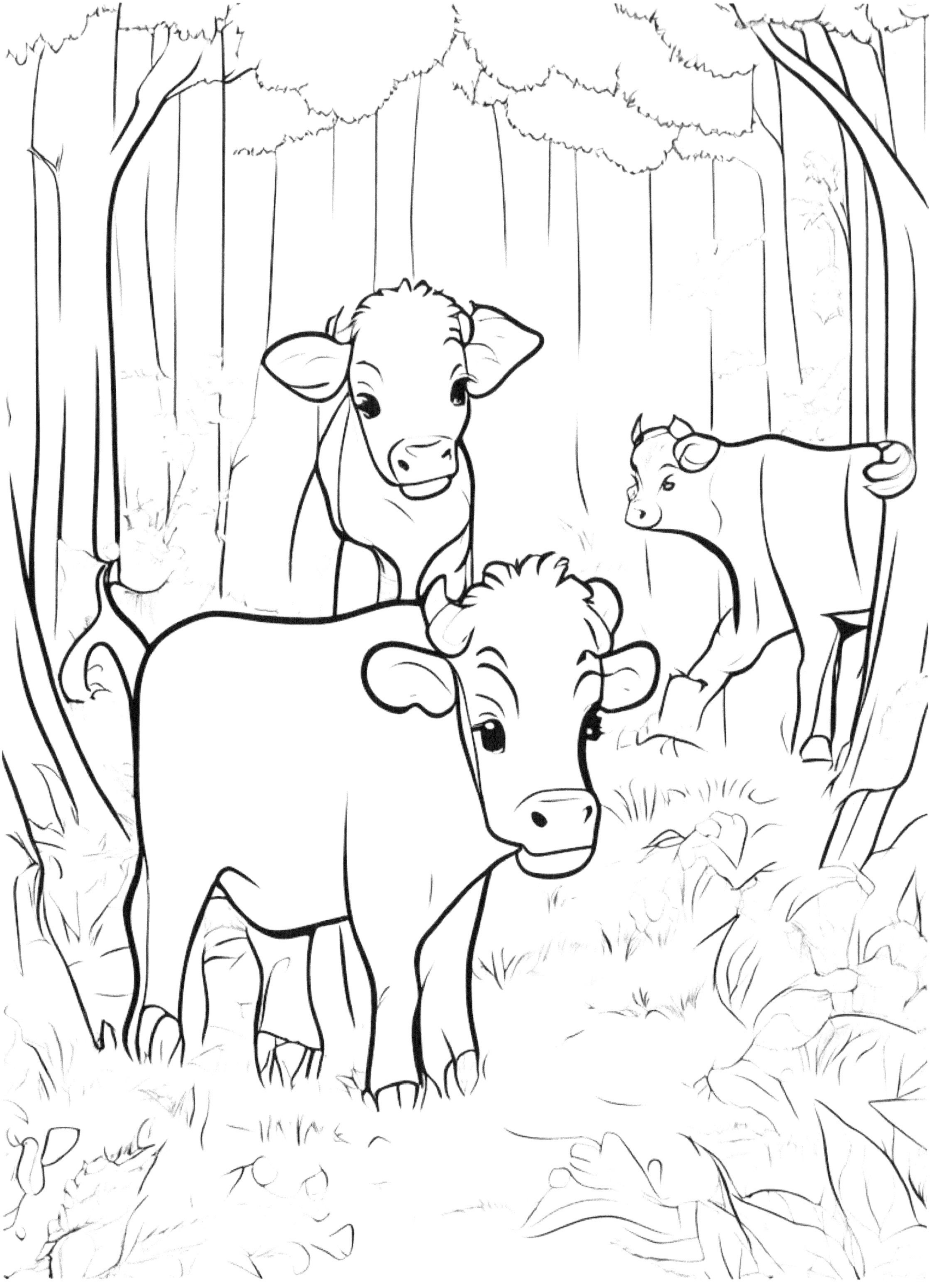

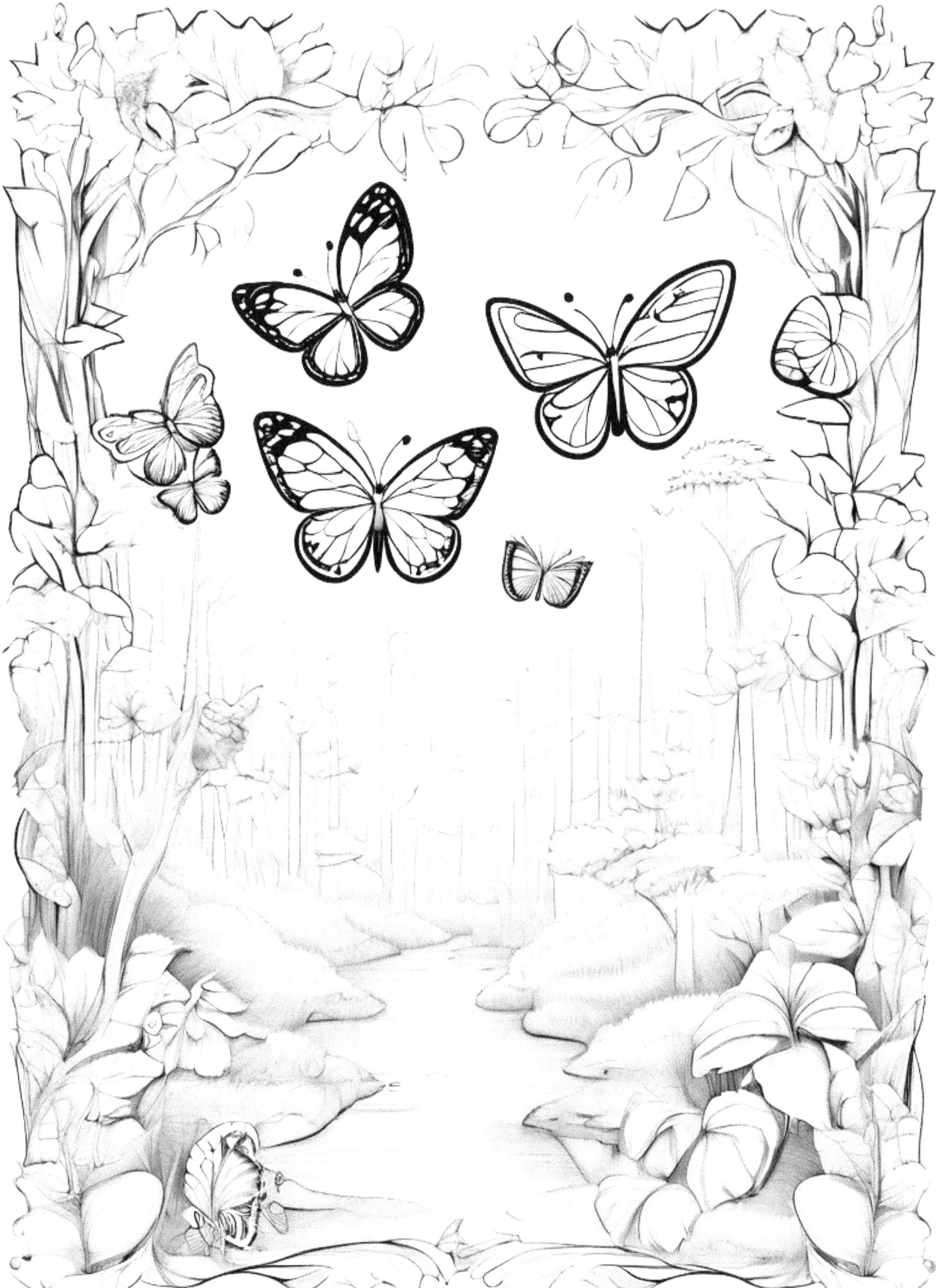

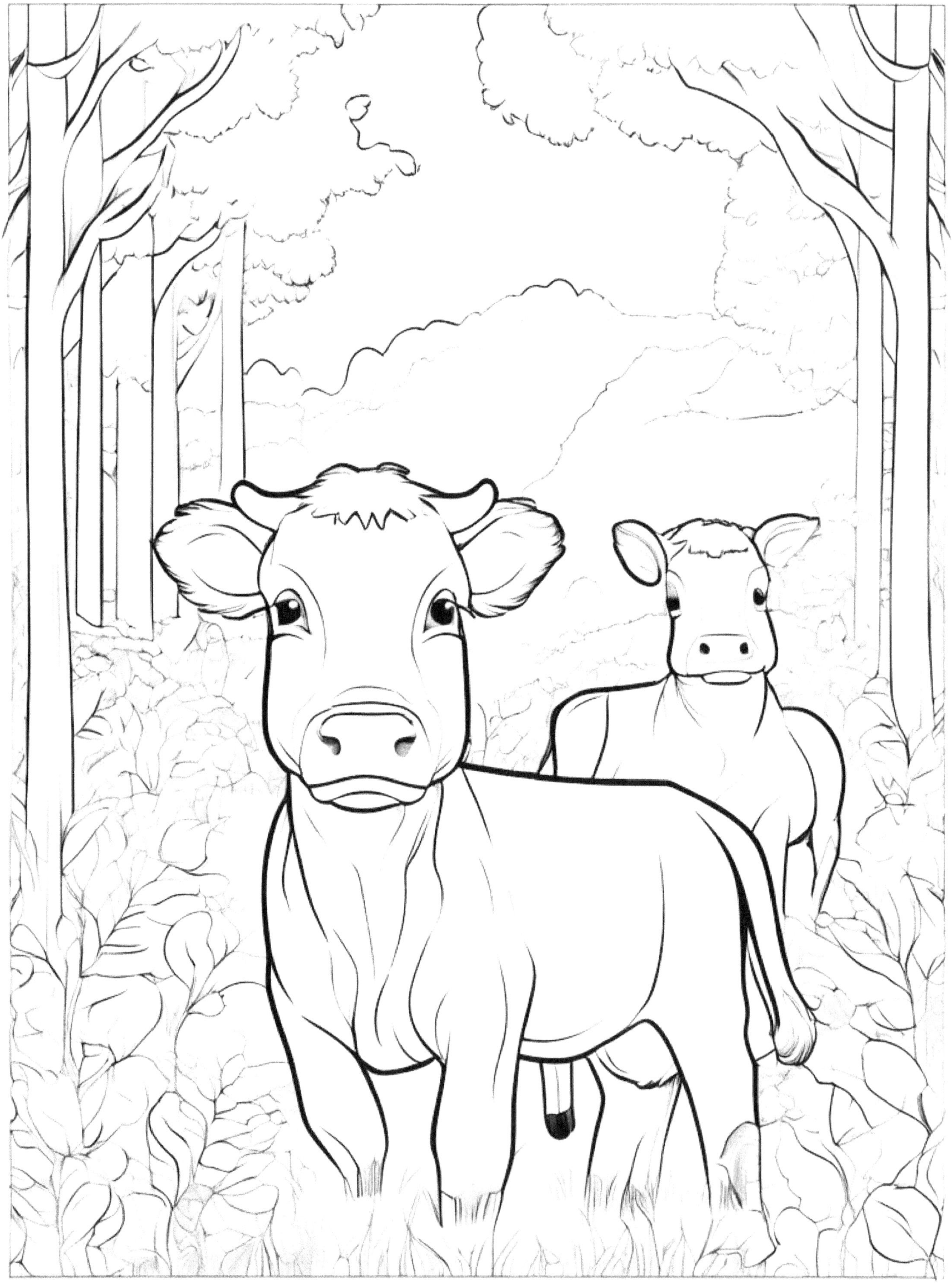

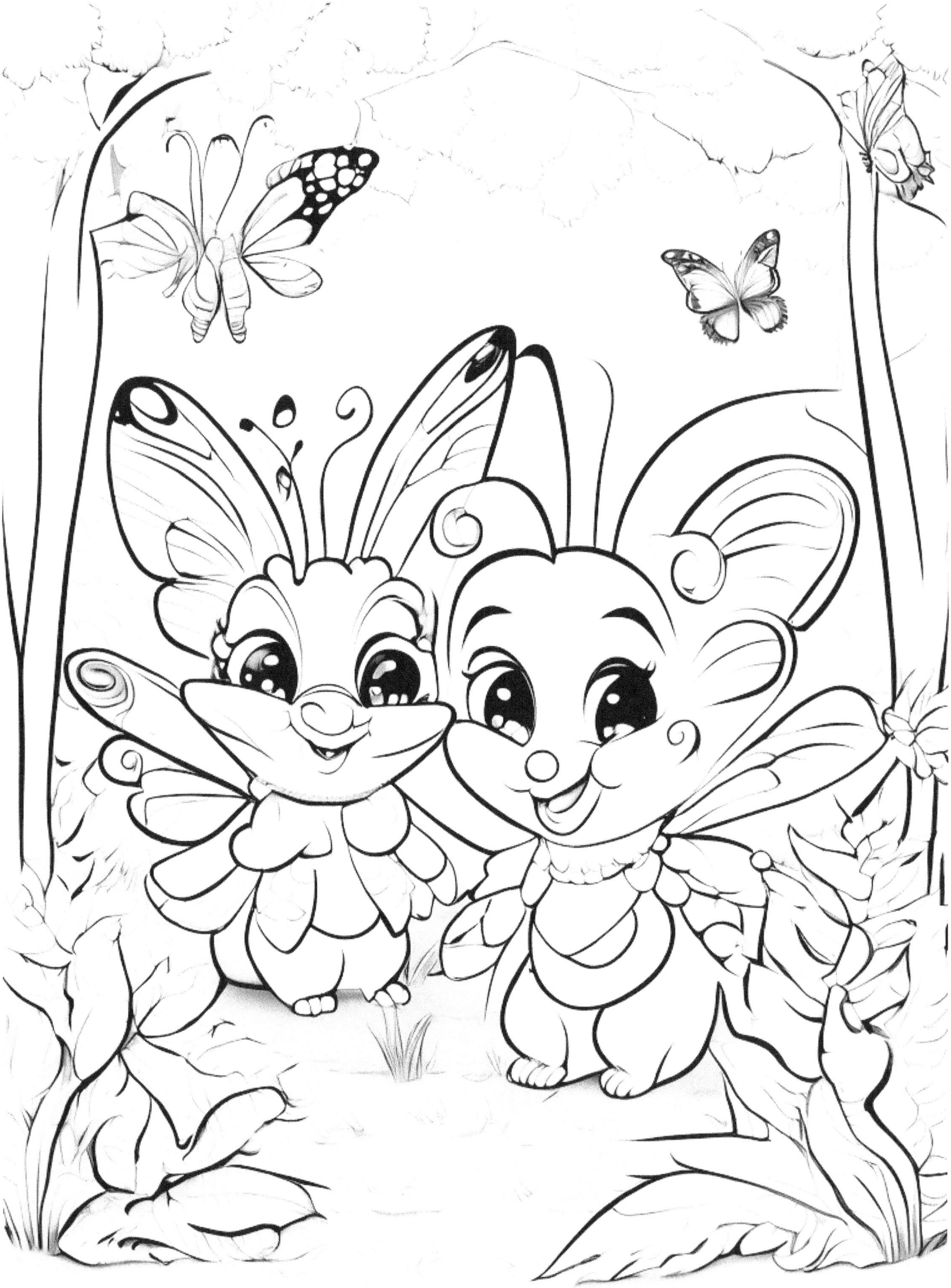

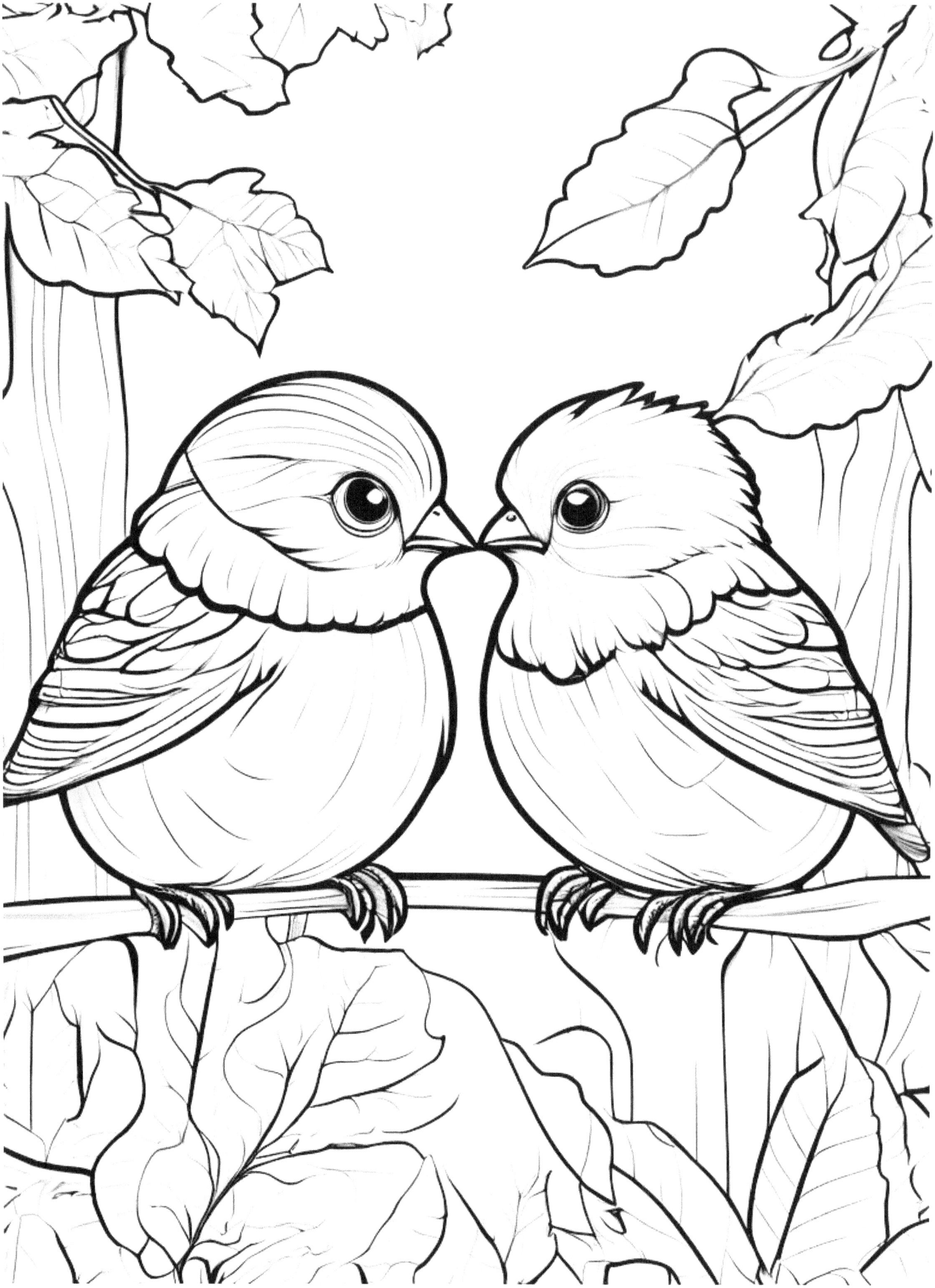

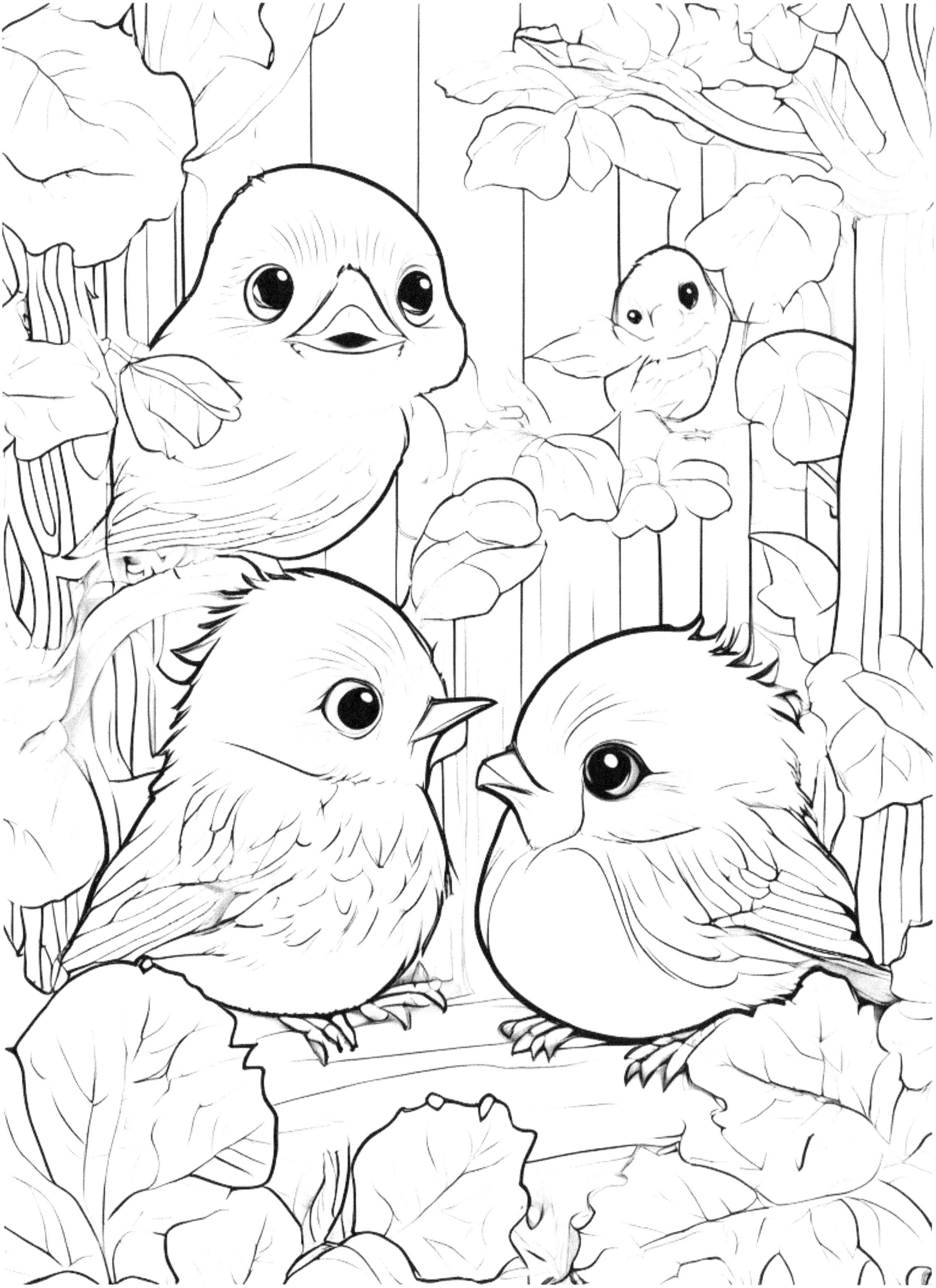

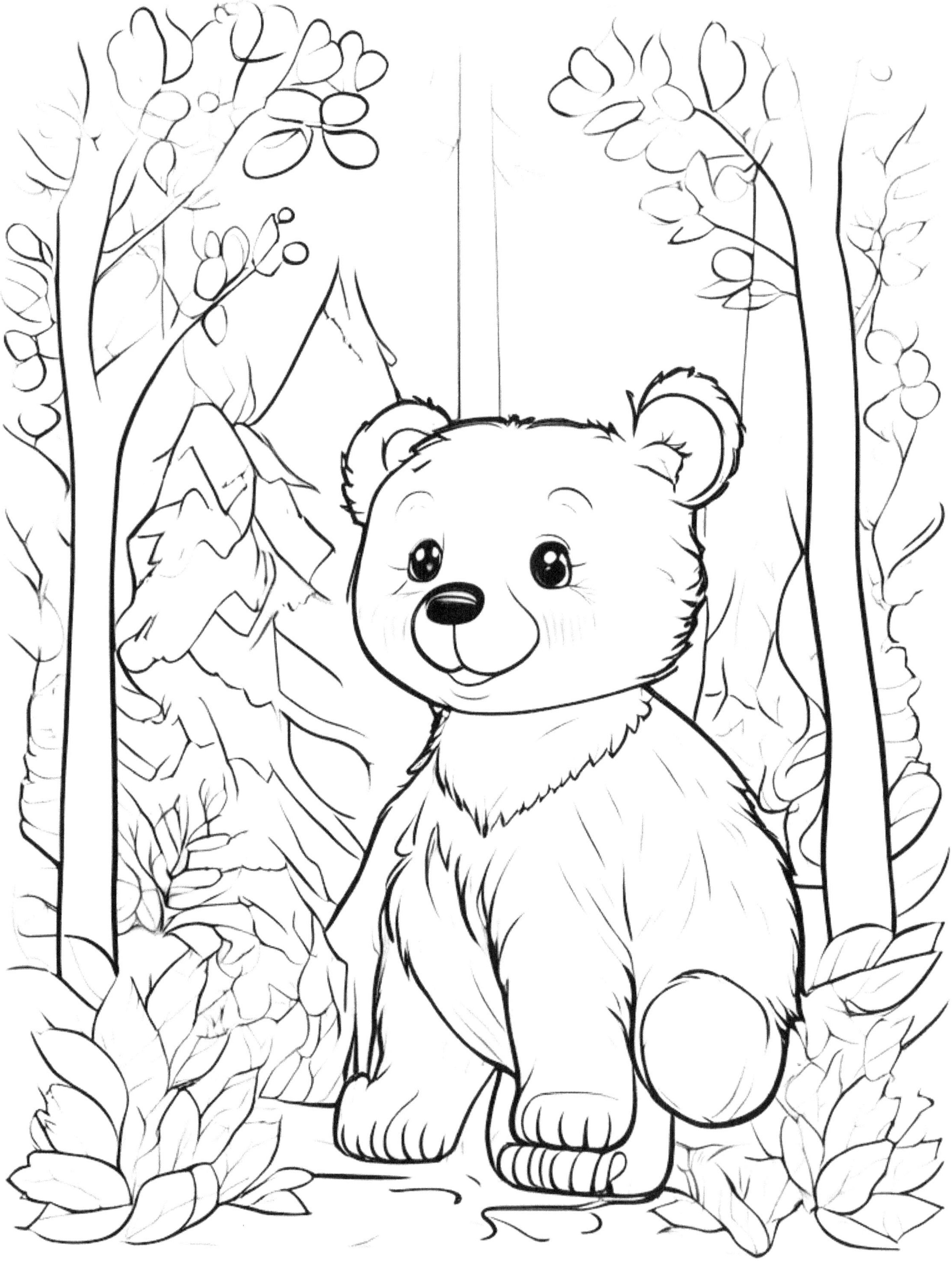

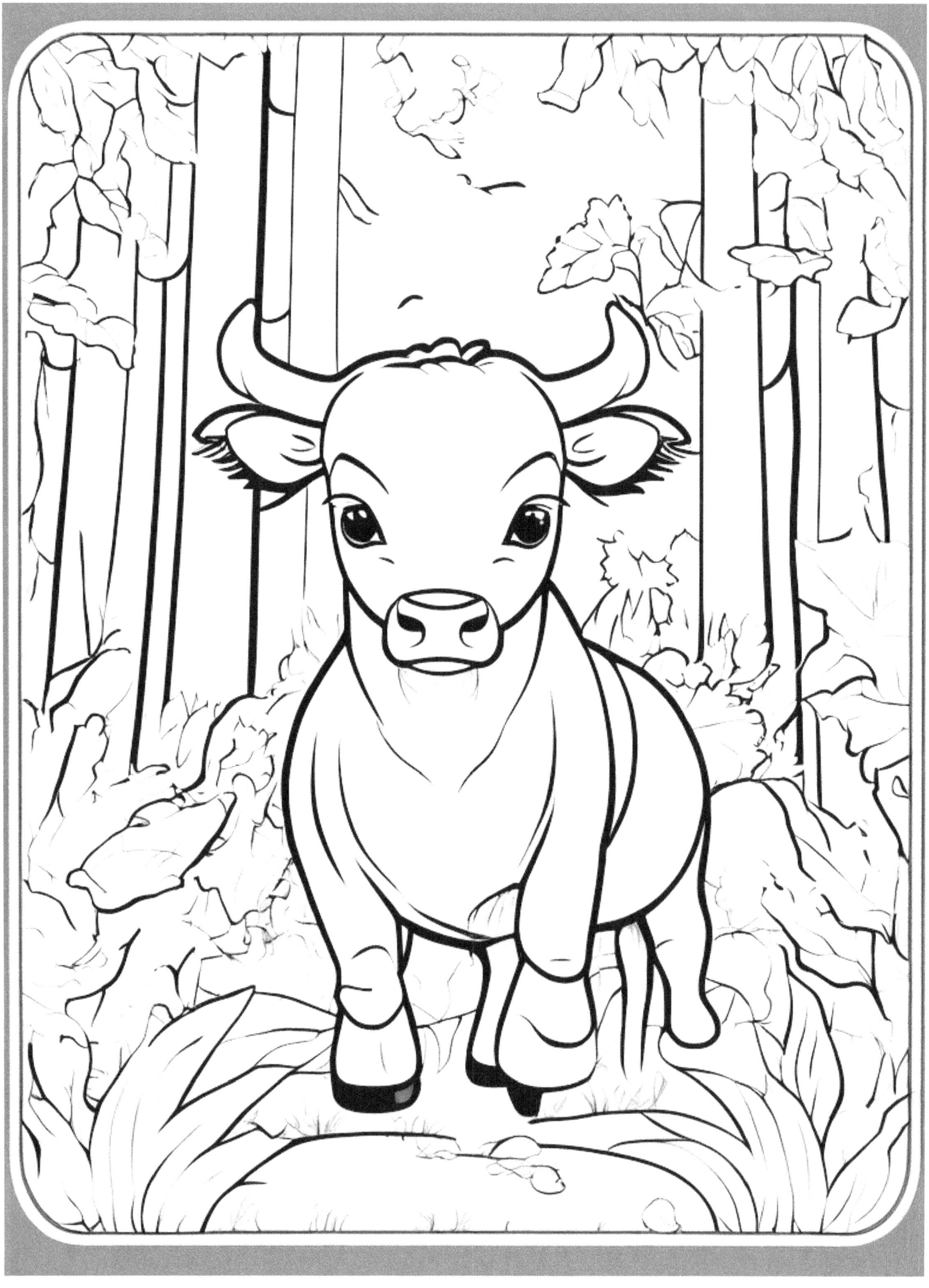

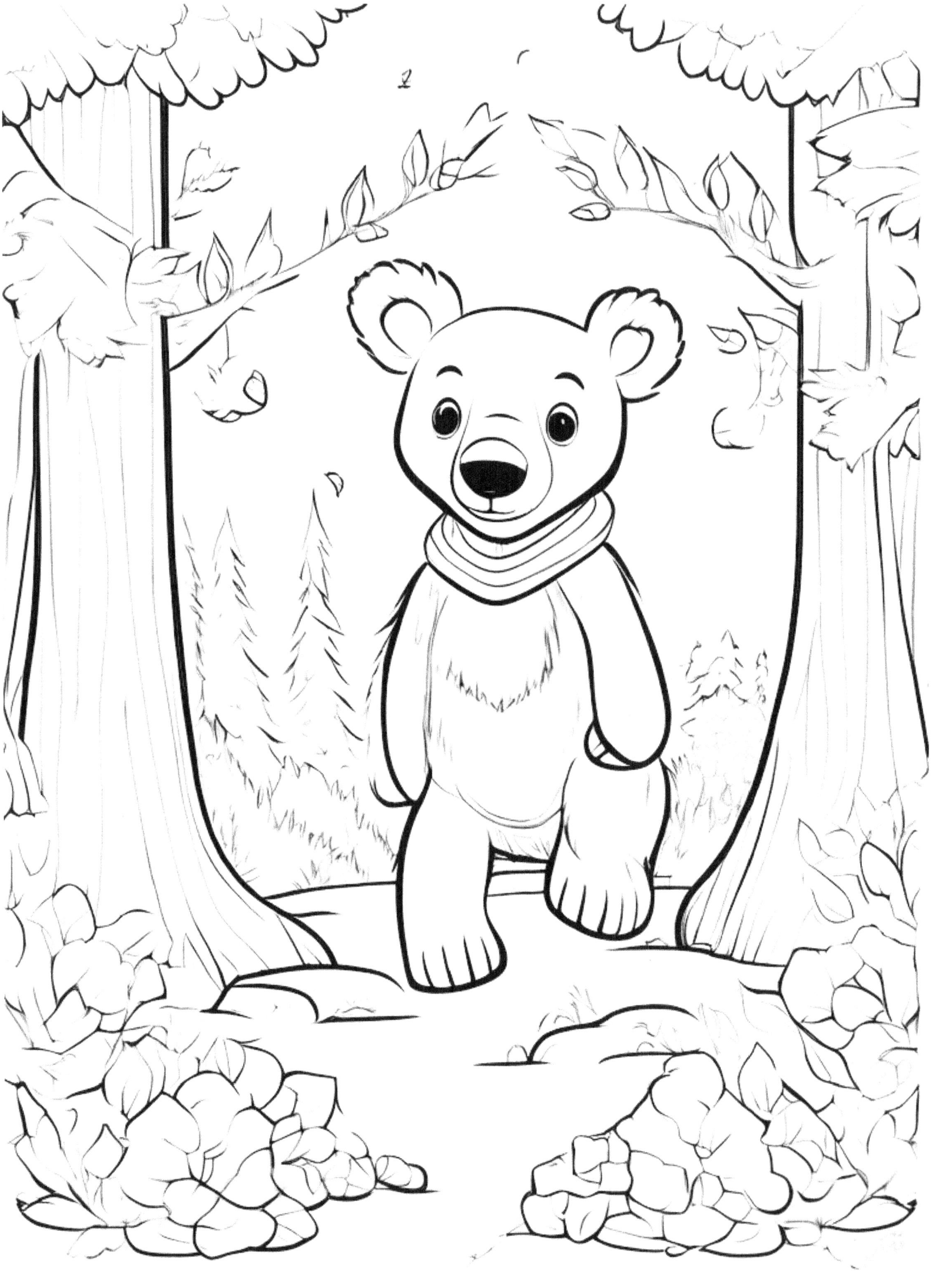

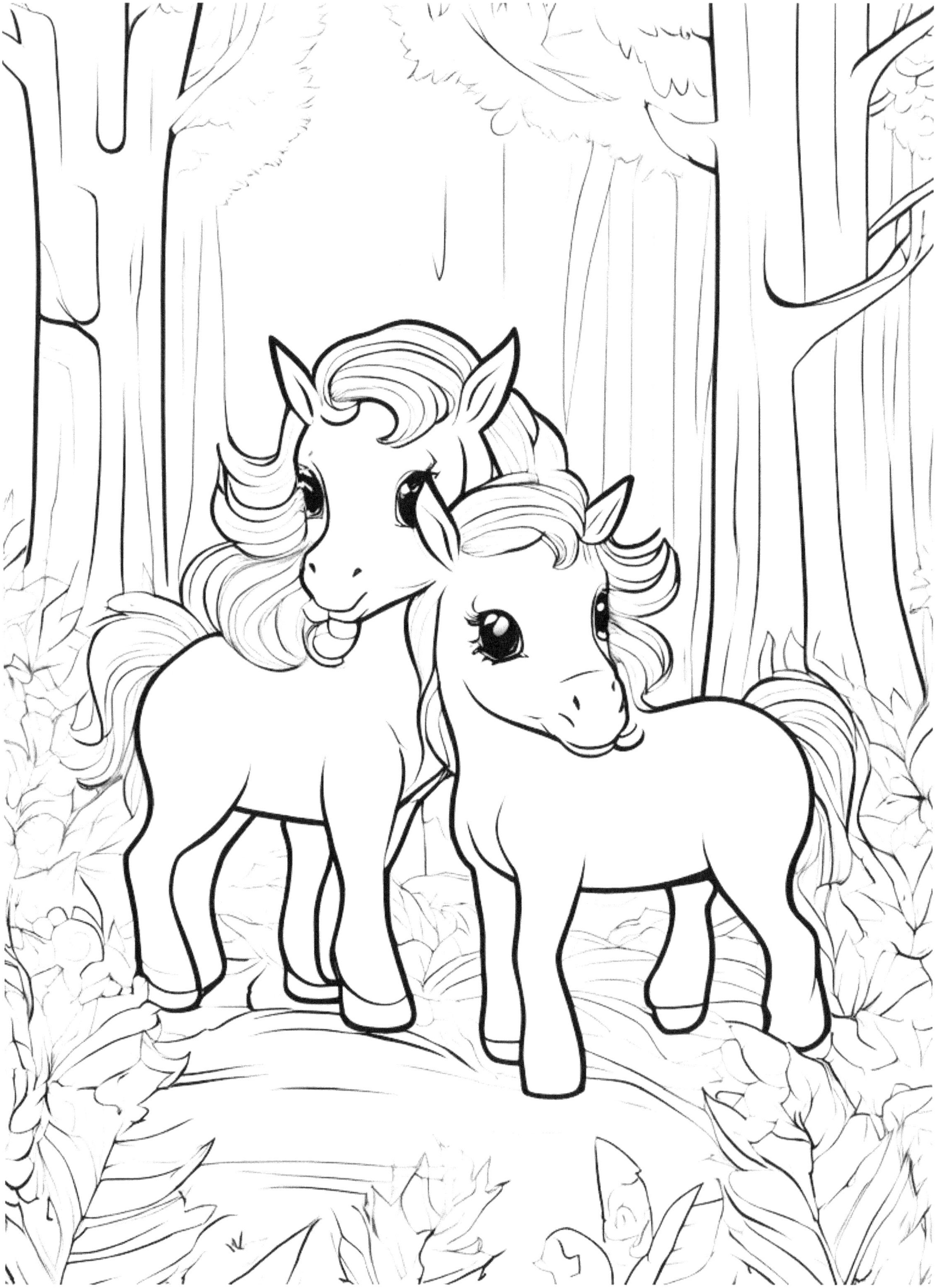

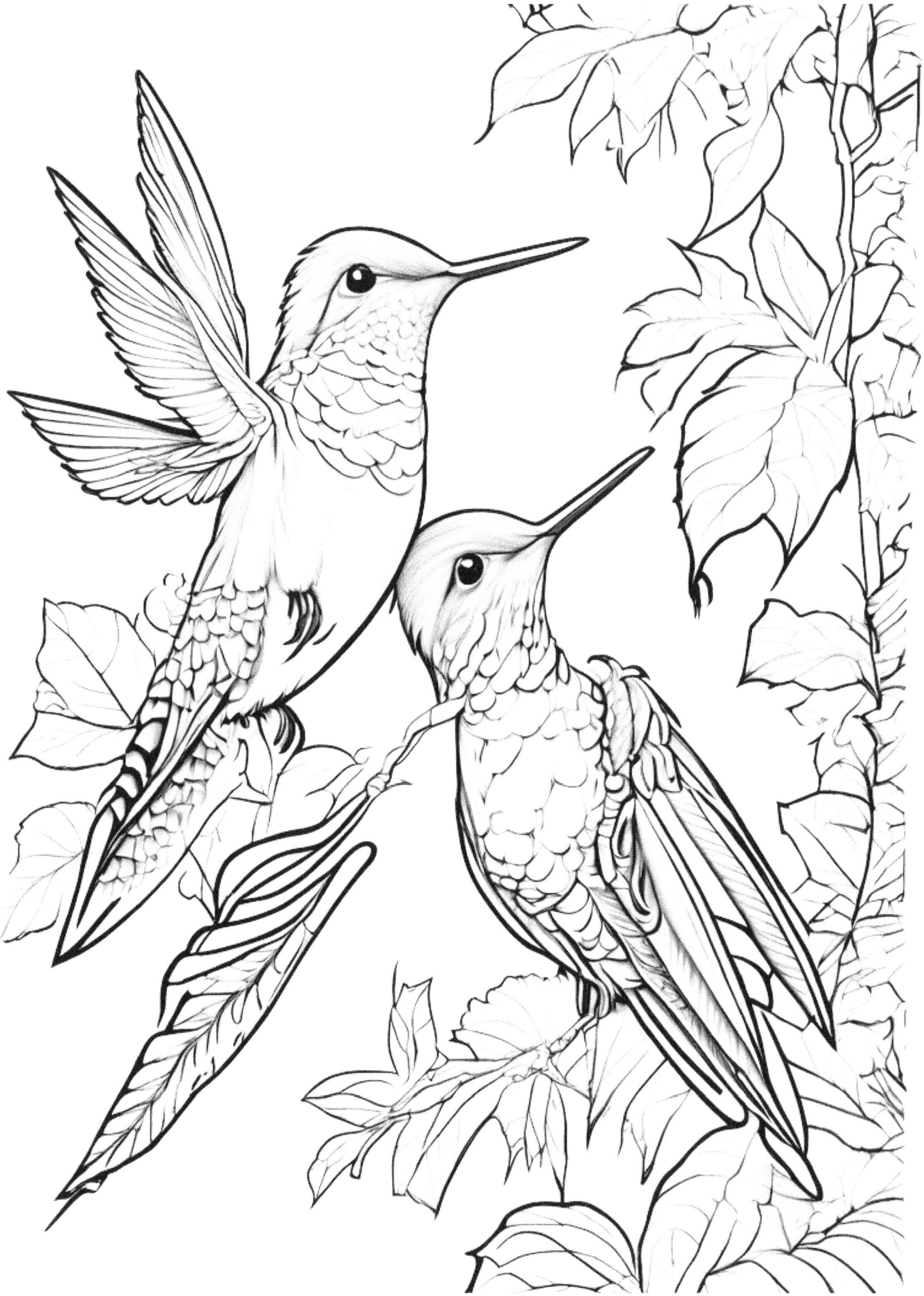

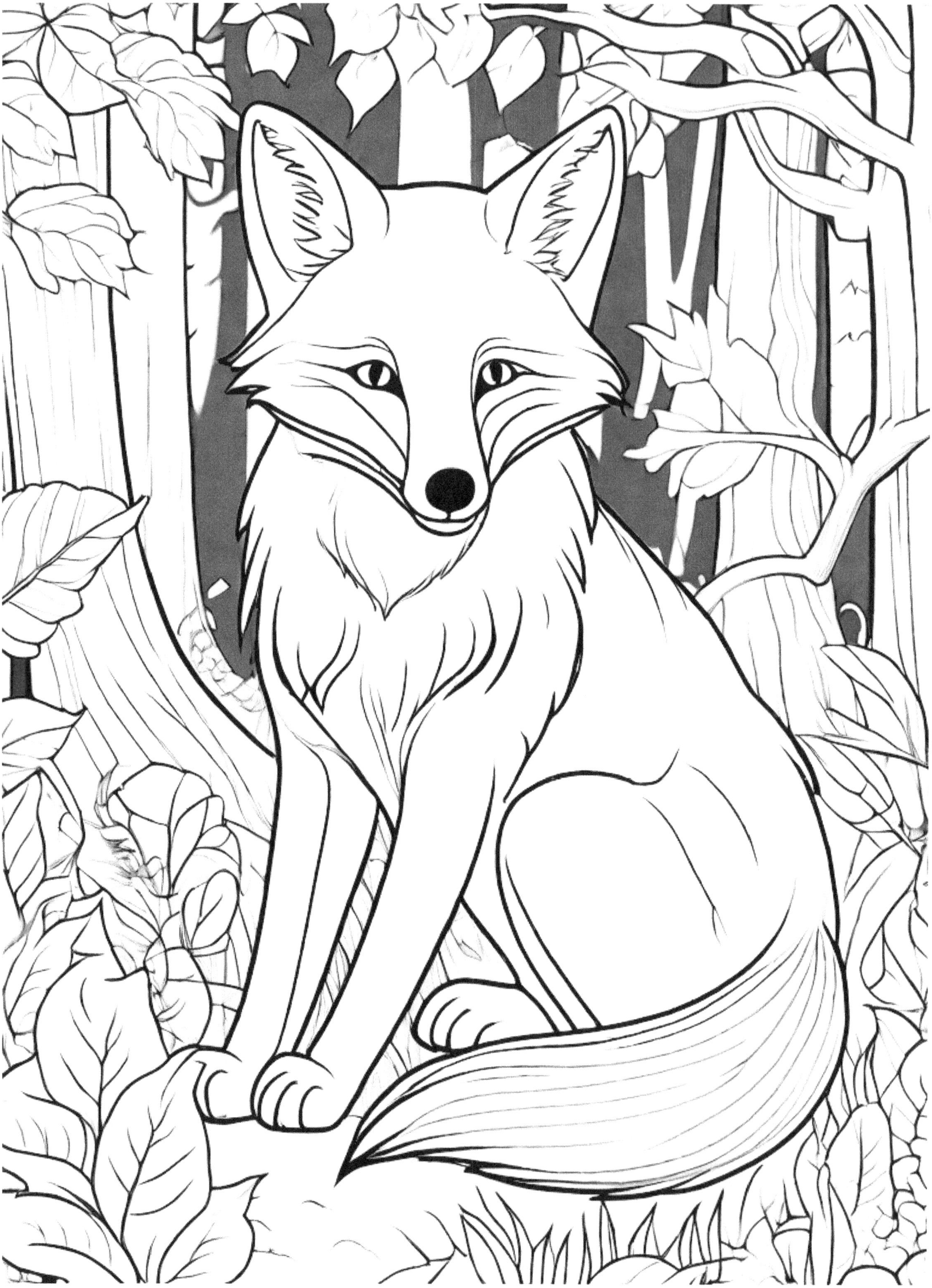

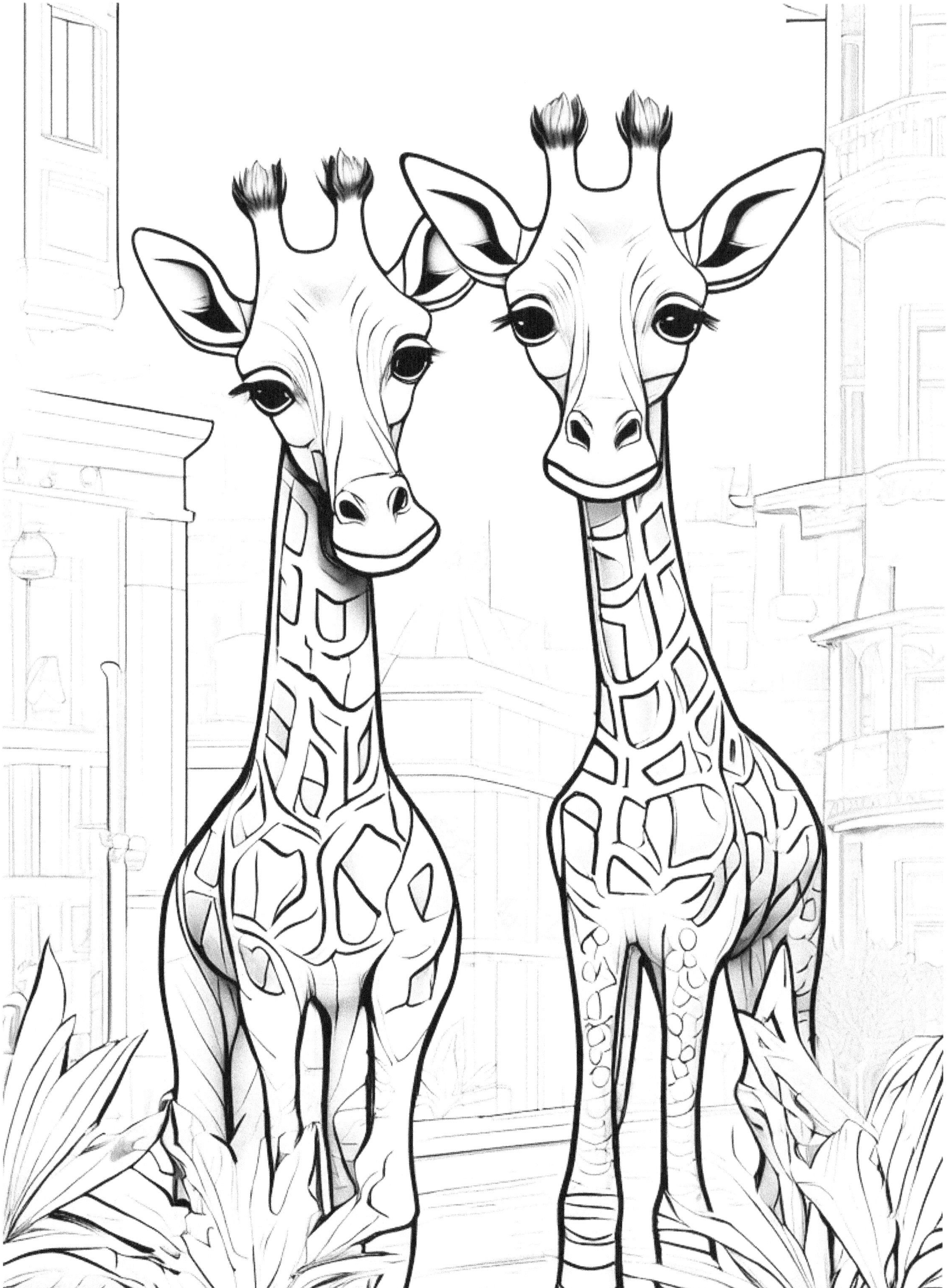

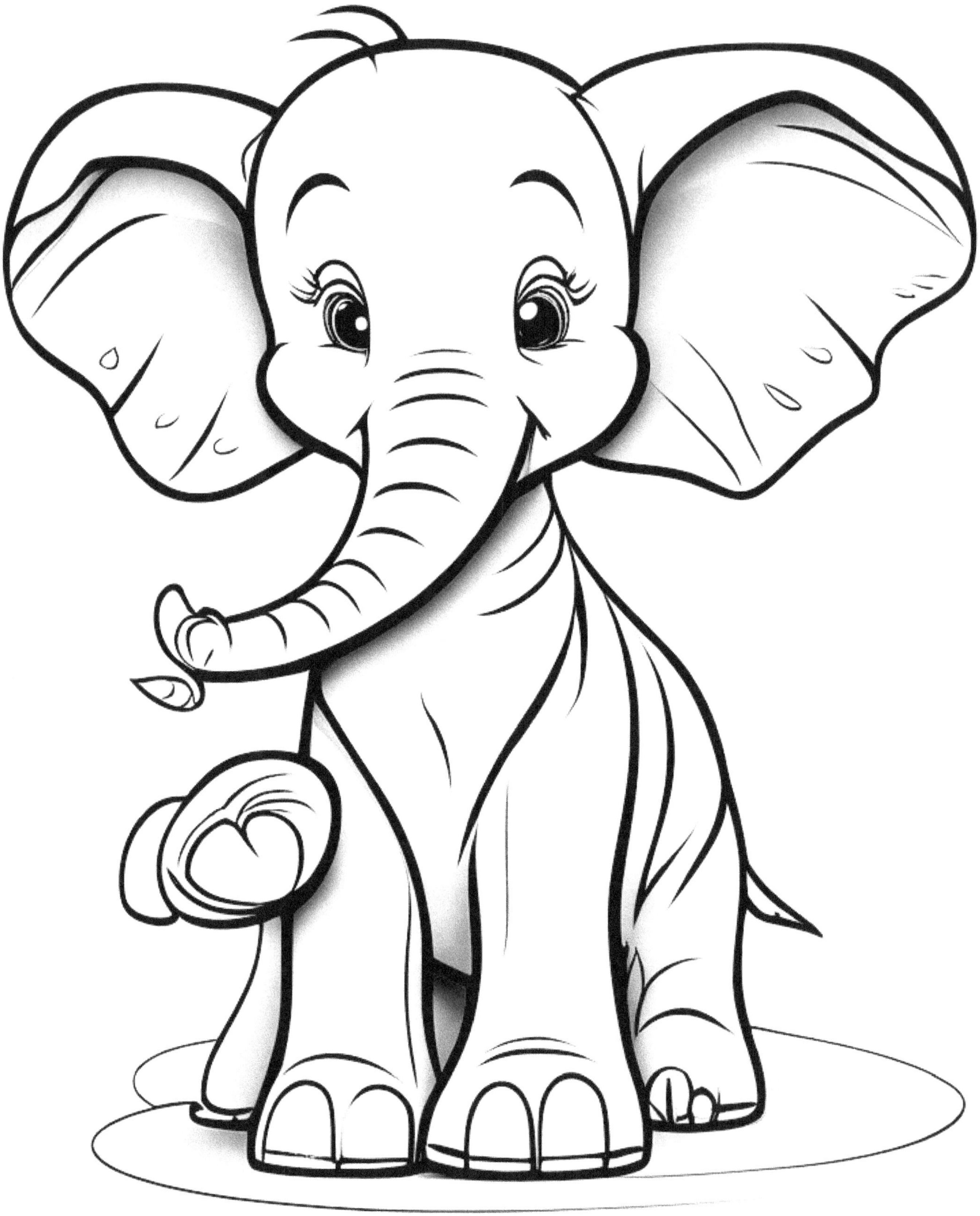

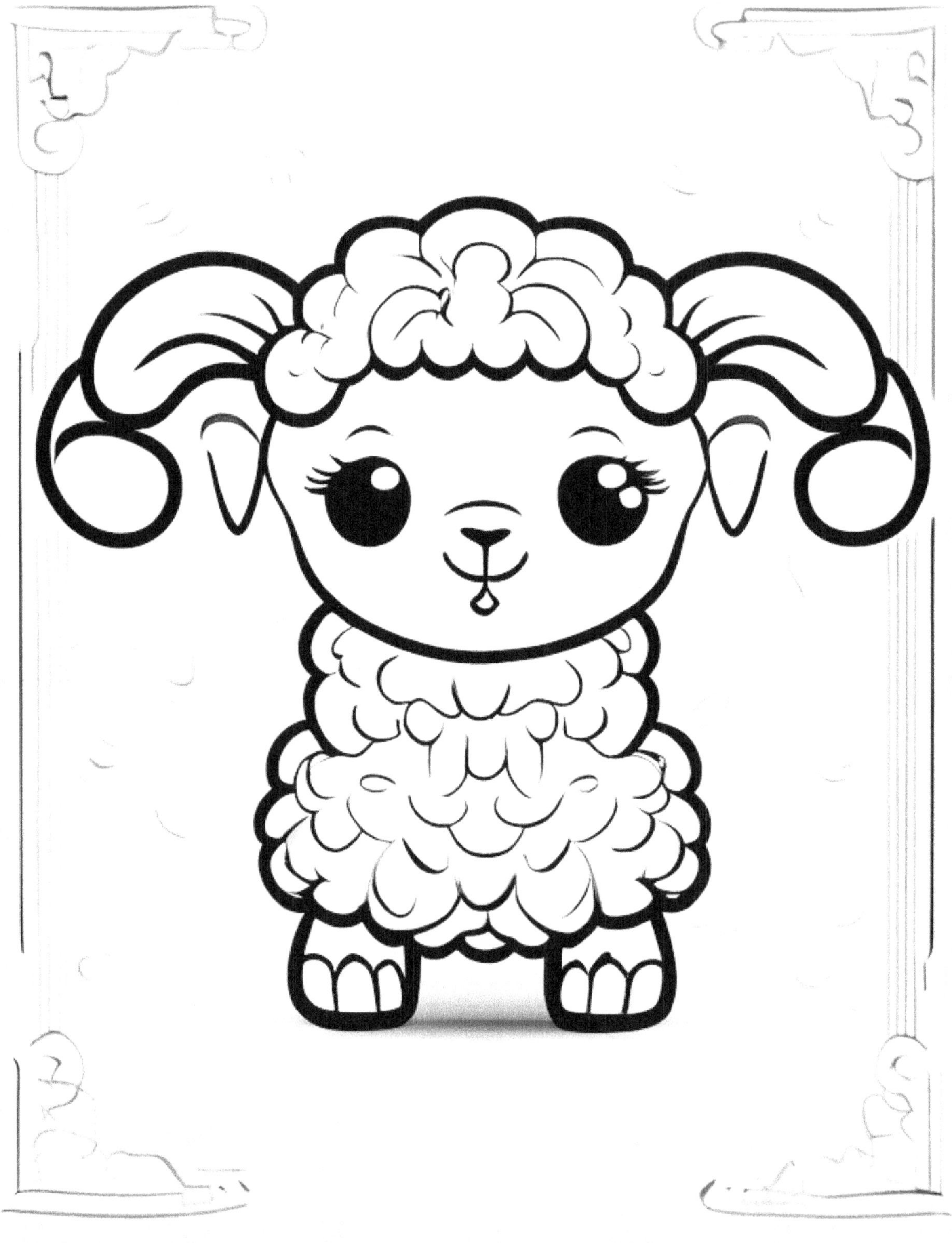

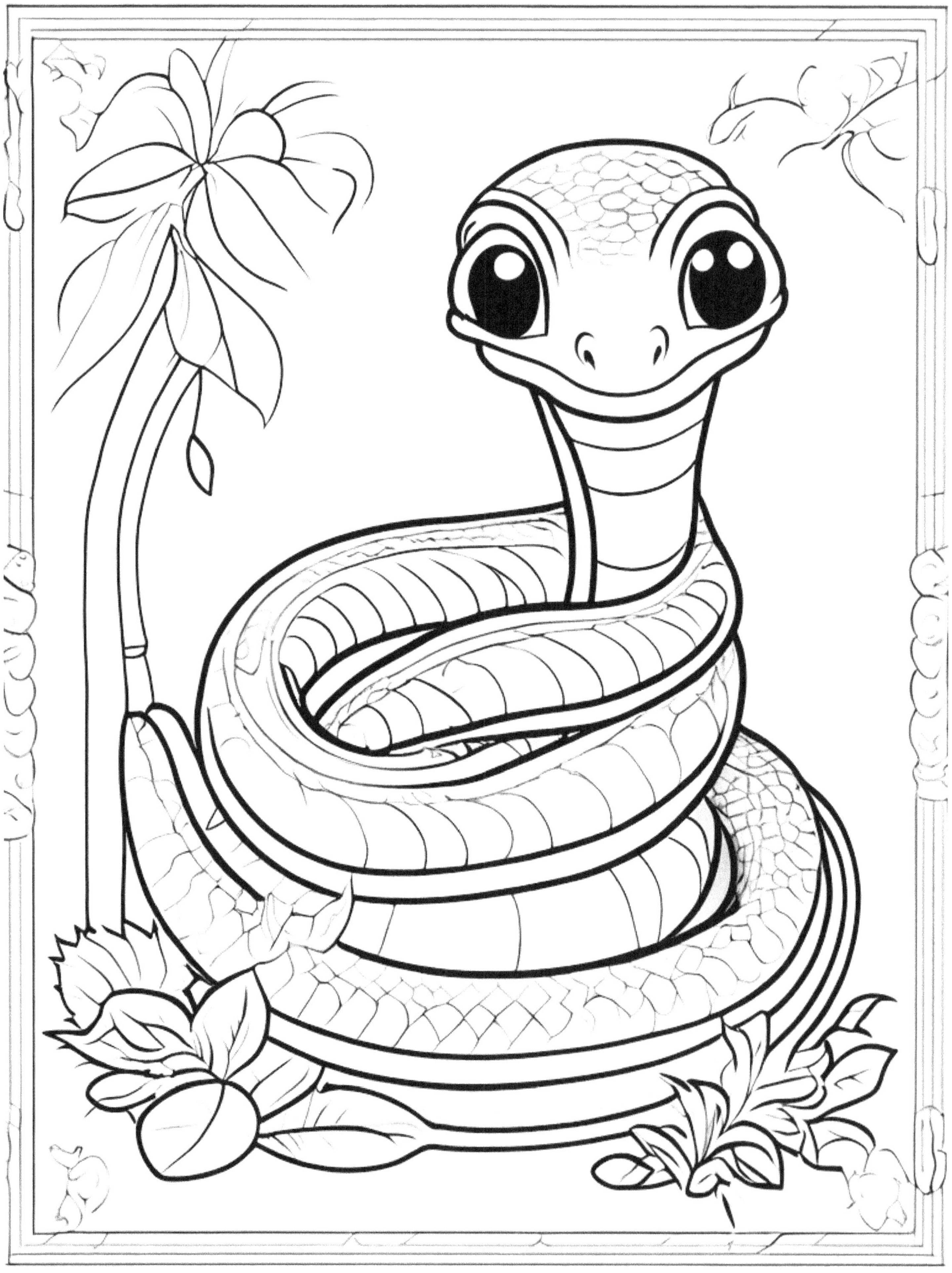

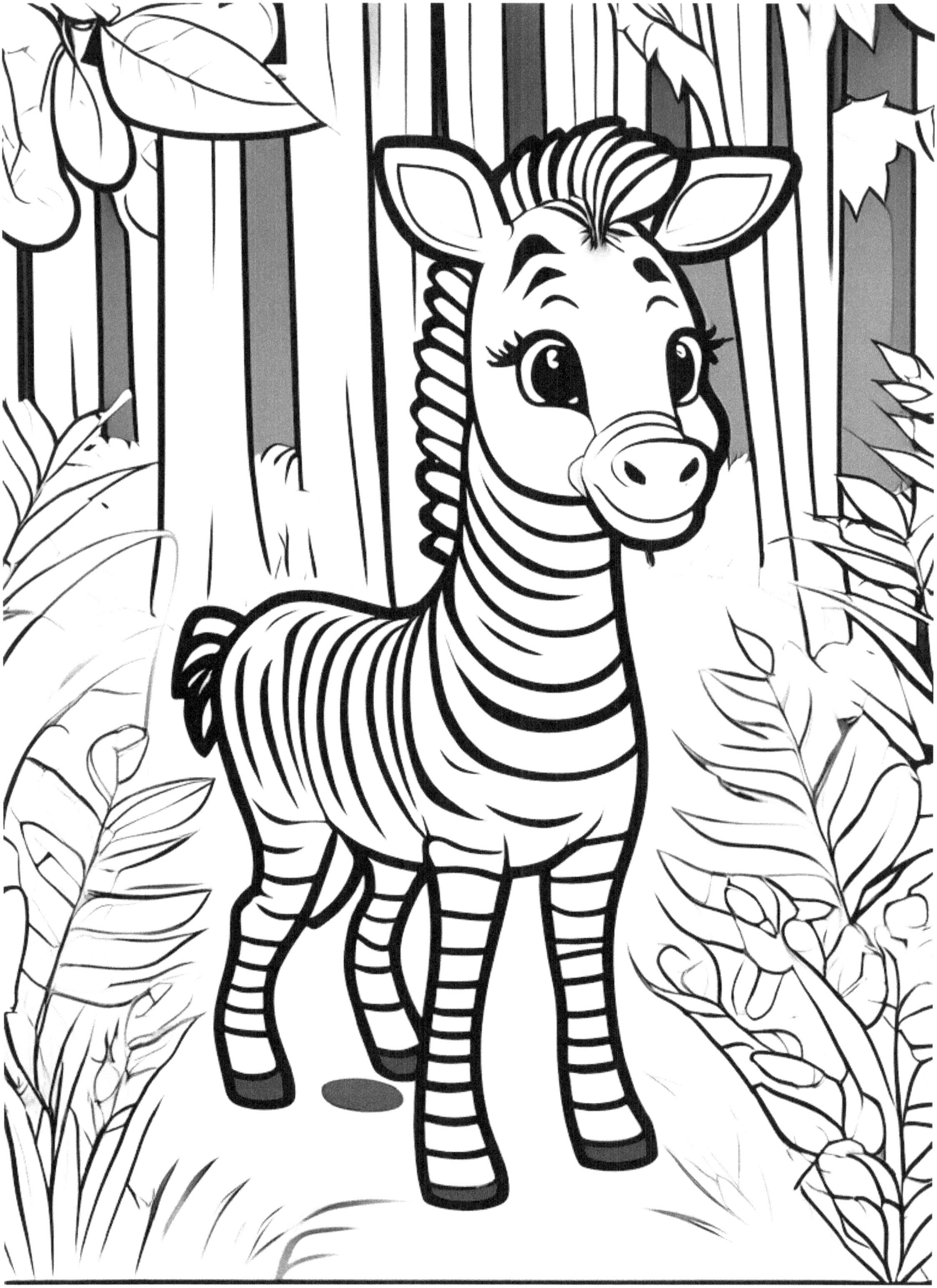

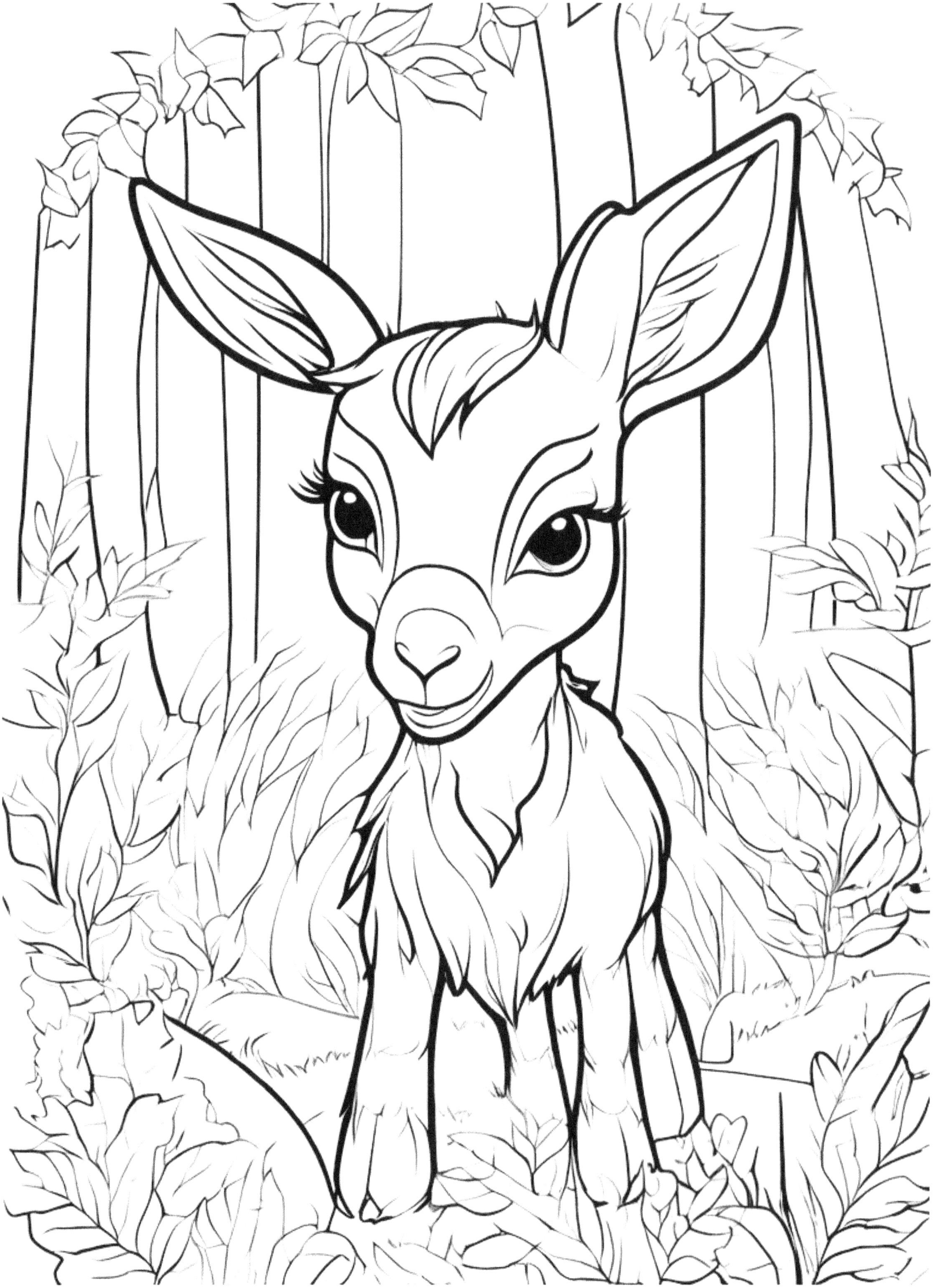

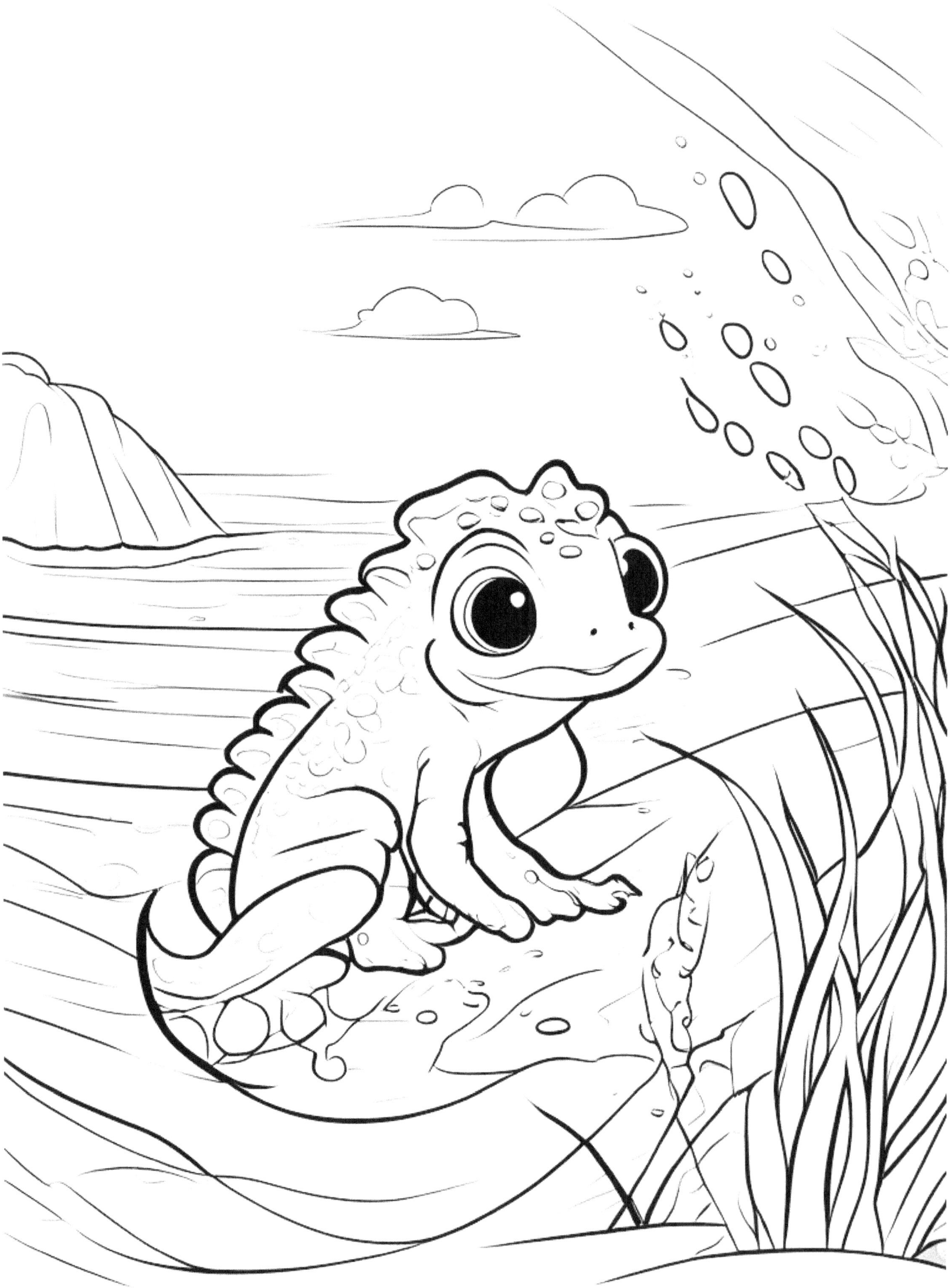

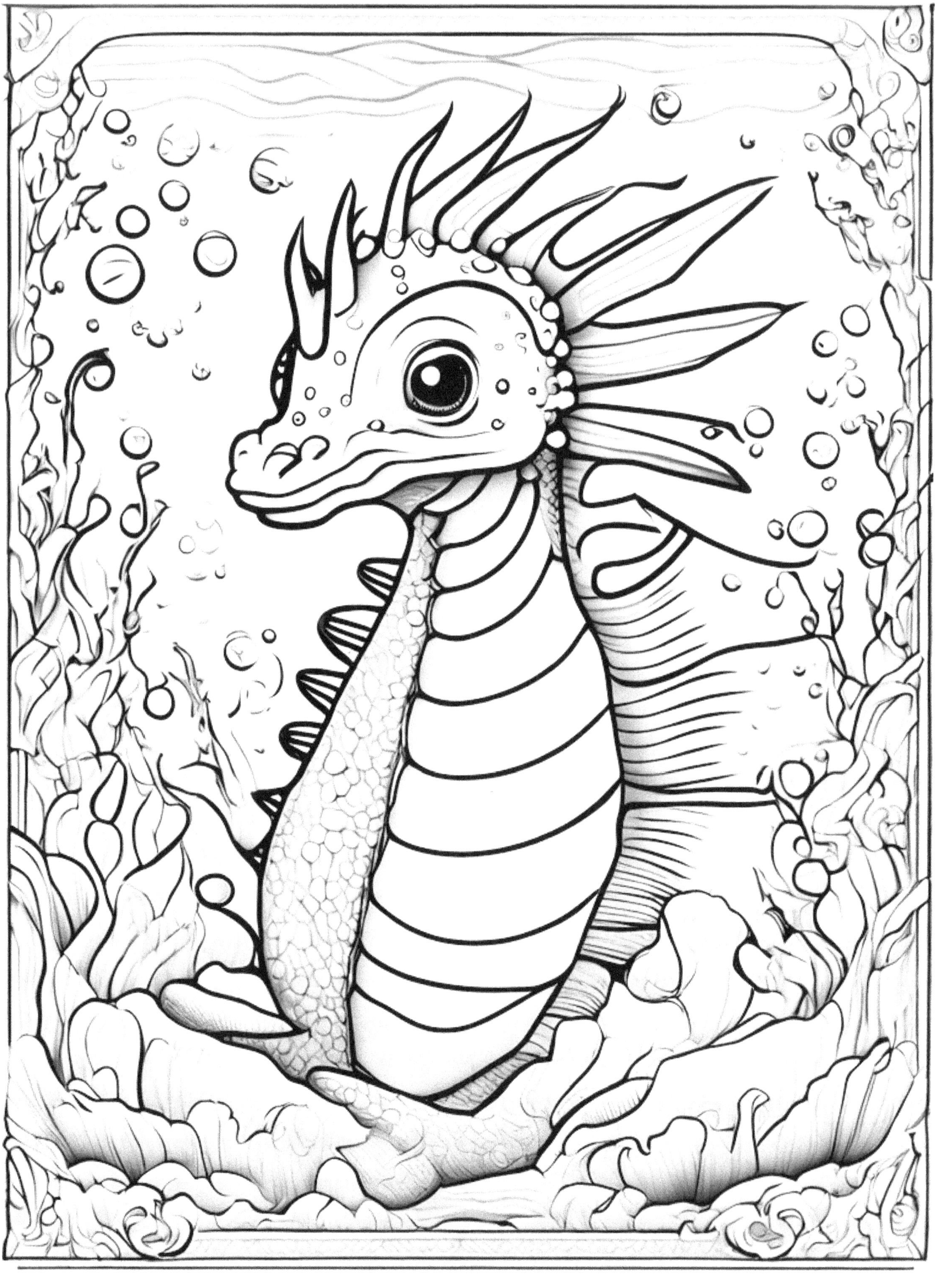

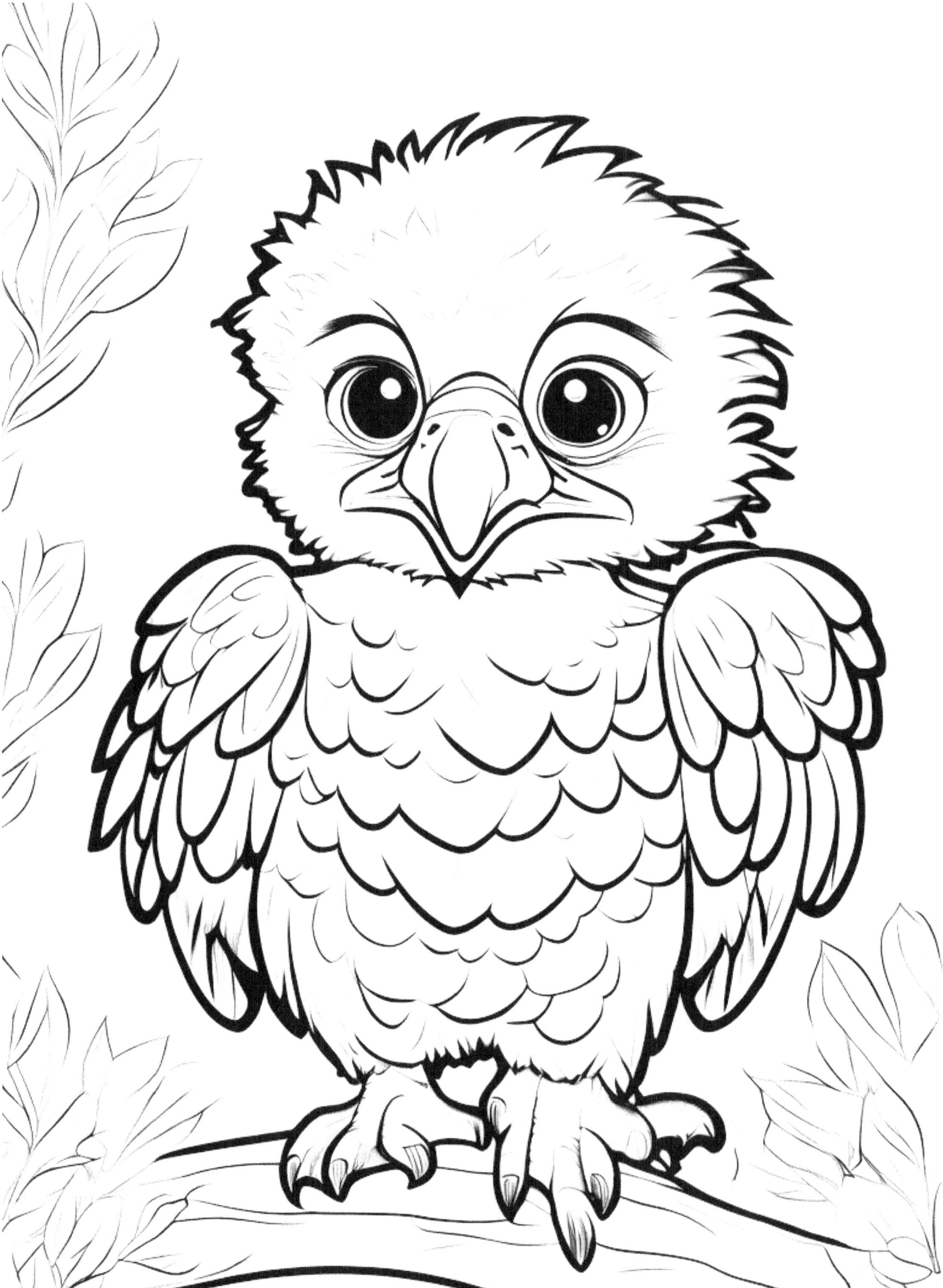

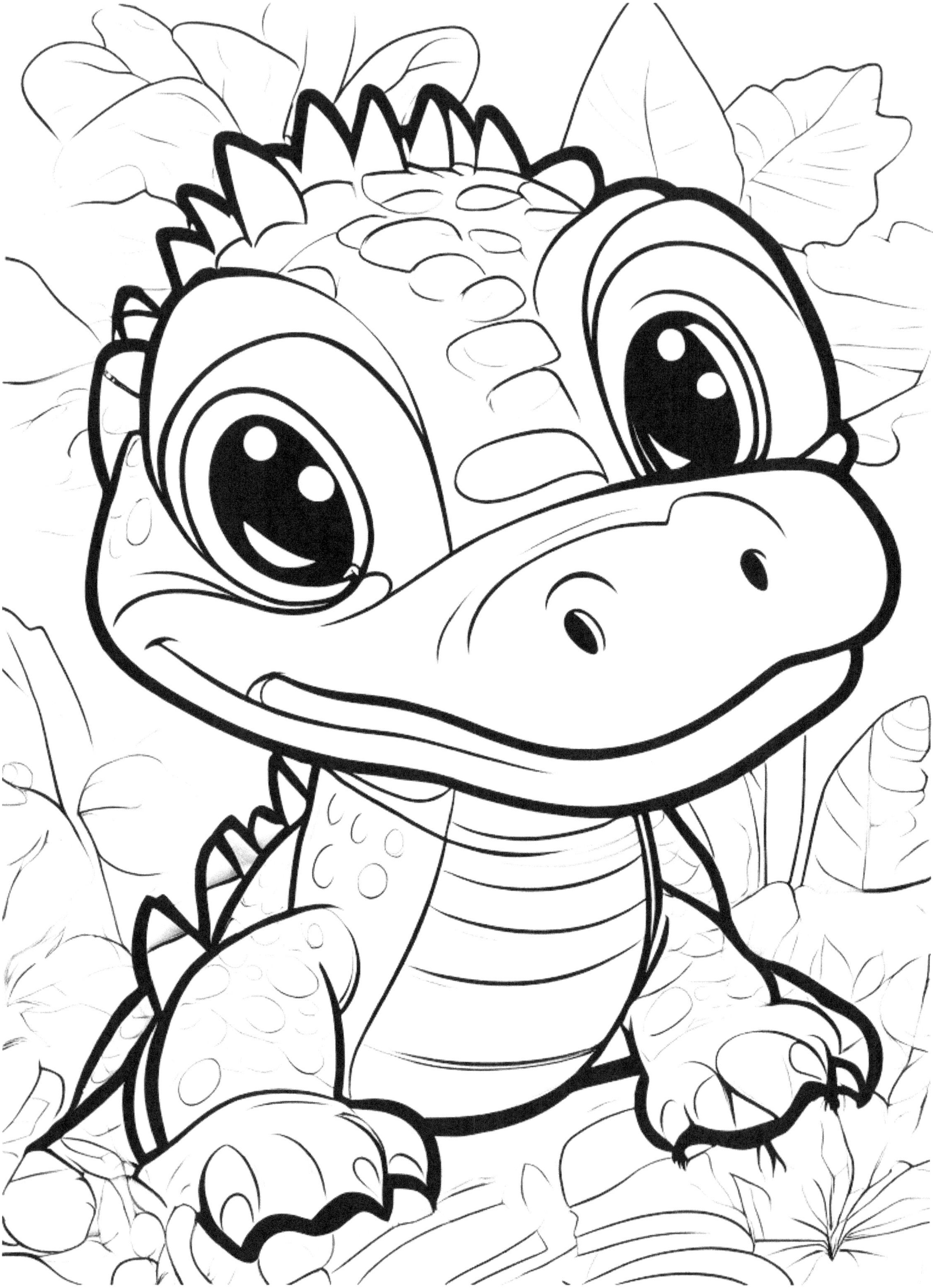

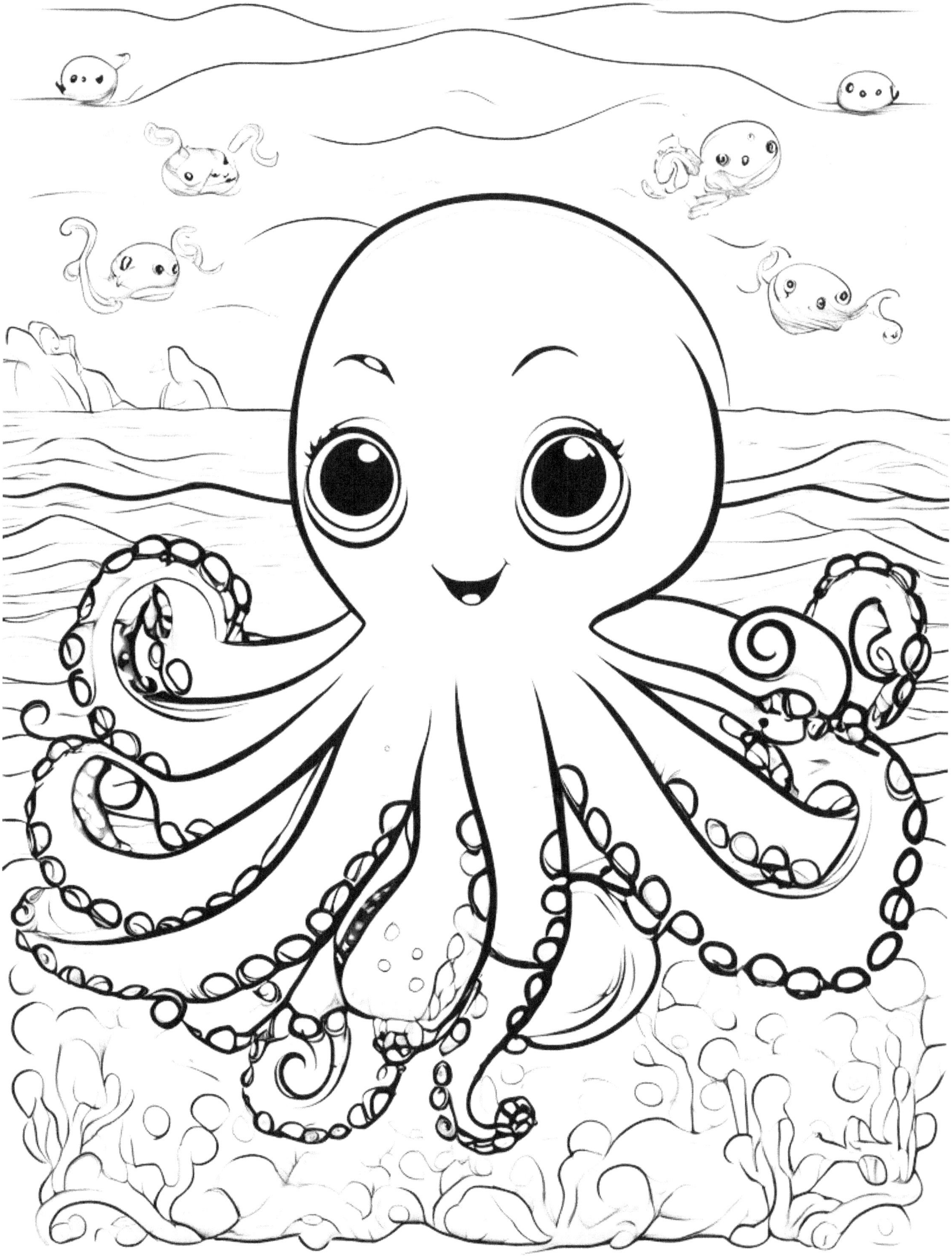

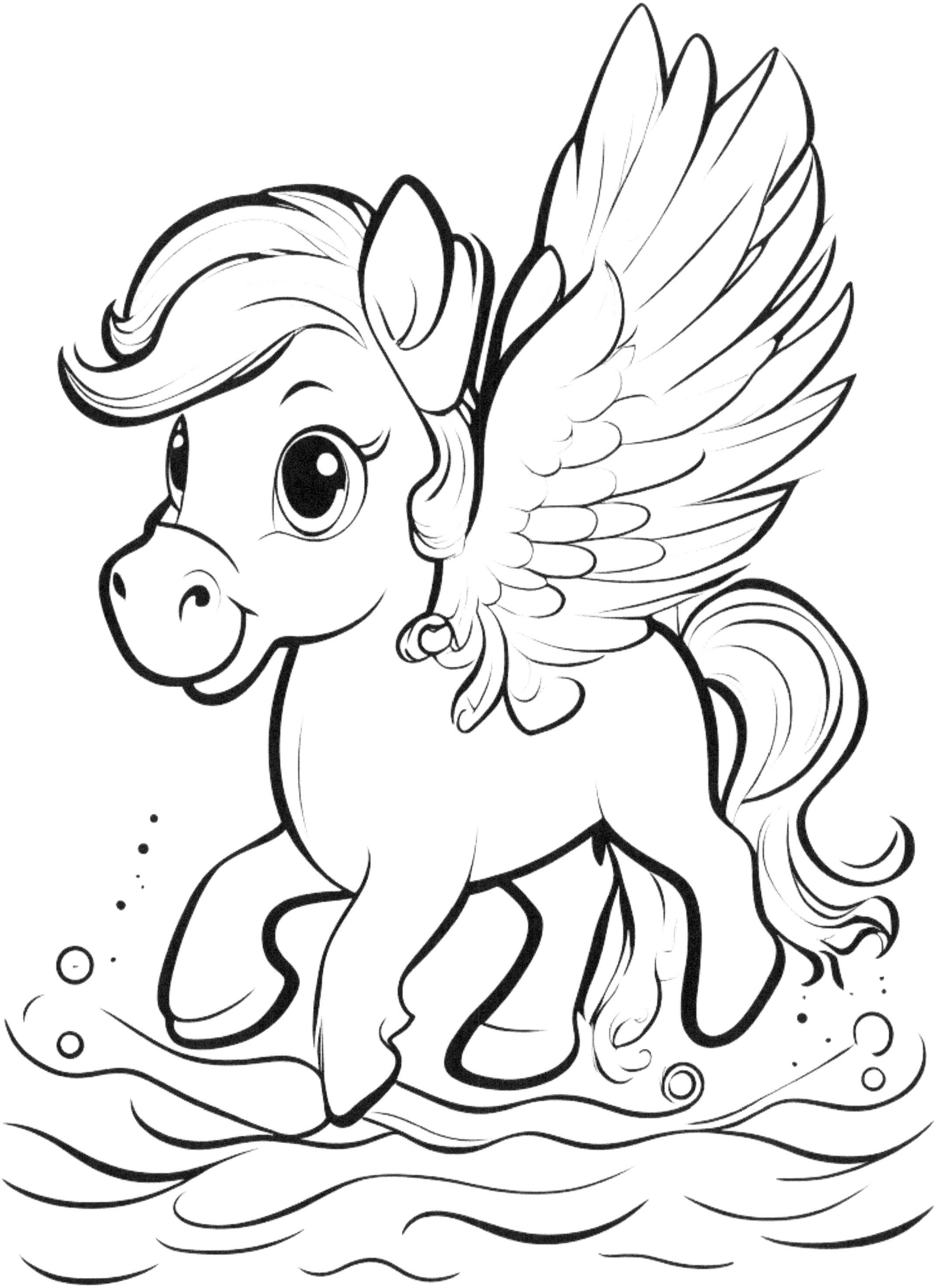

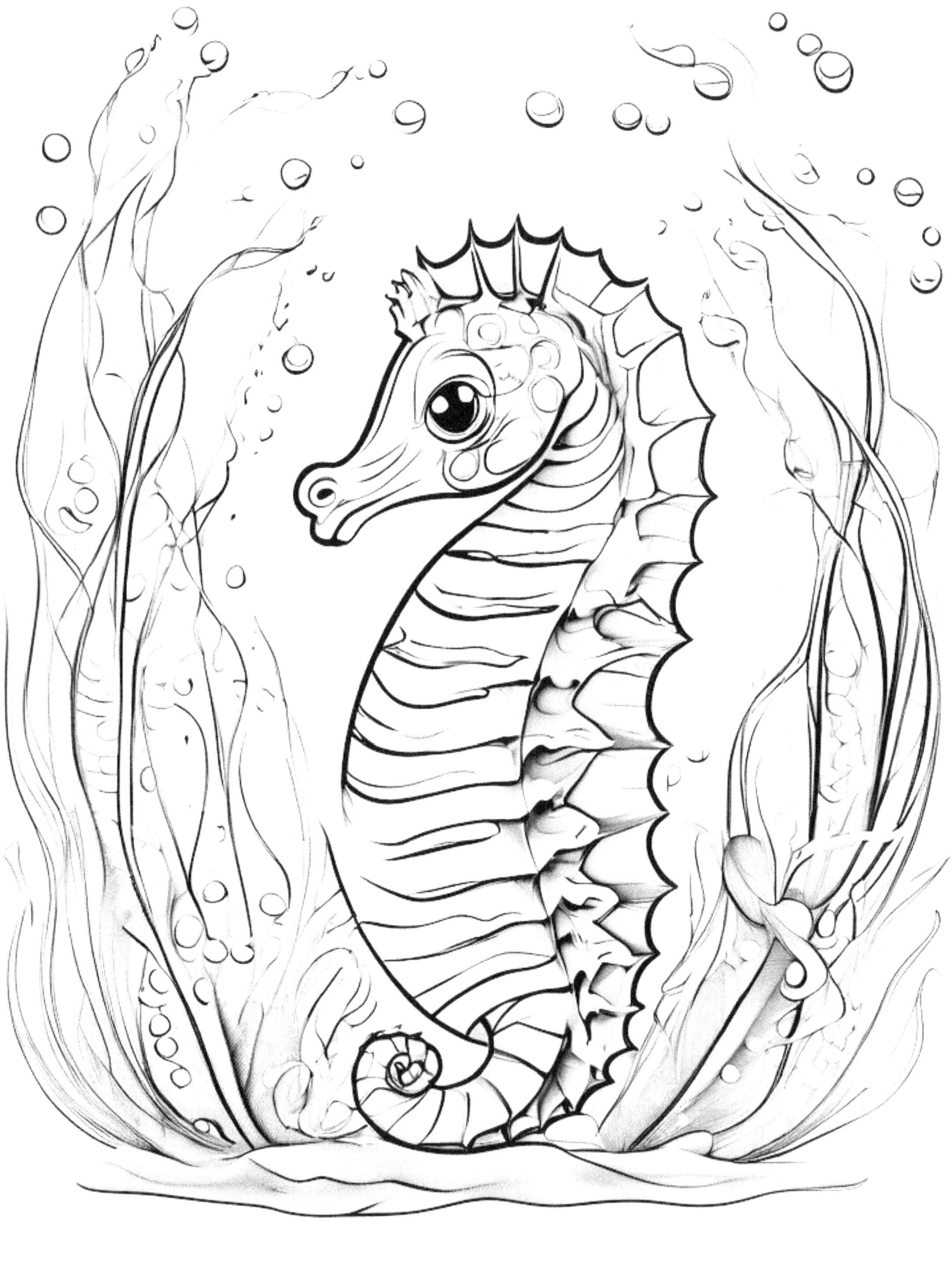

www.ingramcontent.com/pod-product-compliance
Lightning Source LLC
Chambersburg PA
CBHW082225290526
45794CB00009B/3681
* 9 7 9 8 8 7 3 3 3 8 3 9 9 *